The Drunka or Down with

A Melodrama

Book, music and lyrics by
Brian J. Burton

Based on the 19th century version by
W. H. Smith and "A Gentleman"

Samuel French — London
New York — Sydney — Toronto — Hollywood

© 1968 BY BRIAN J BURTON

Rights of Performance by Amateurs are controlled by Samuel French Ltd, 52 Fitzroy Street, London W1P 6JR, and they, or their authorized agents, issue licences to amateurs on payment of a fee. **It is an infringement of the Copyright to give any performance or public reading of the play before the fee has been paid and the licence issued.**

The Royalty Fee indicated below is subject to contract and subject to variation at the sole discretion of Samuel French Ltd.

> Basic fee for each and every
> performance by amateurs   Code L
> in the British Isles

The publication of this play does not imply that it is necessarily available for performance by amateurs or professionals, either in the British Isles or Overseas. Amateurs and professionals considering a production are strongly advised in their own interests to apply to the appropriate agents for consent before starting rehearsals or booking a theatre or hall.

ISBN 0 573 01625 9

Please see page x for further copyright information

Printed and bound in Great Britain by
J. W. Arrowsmith Ltd. Bristol

CHARACTERS

The Drunkard or **Down With Demon Drink!** was first presented at the Swan Theatre Worcester, on December 14th, 1968 with the following cast: —

Mrs Wilson	Margaret Callow
Mary Wilson	Mary Cooke
Squire Cribbs	Frank Bench
Edward Middleton	Ted Cooke
Sophia Spindle	Sonia Davis
William Dowton	Colin Russell
Agnes Dowton	Christine Wargent
Mrs Miller	Jo Kislingbury
Mrs Gates	Beryl Gough
Mrs Stevens	Diana Brooks
Sam Adams	Willie Harrell
The Landlord	Leslie G. Hill
Julia Middleton	Anne Needham
Arden Rencelaw	Tom Chester
An Officer of the Law	Luke Albarin

Villagers, etc.: Susan Townsend, Adele Head, Rosemary Ratcliffe, Adelaide Murray, Brenda Wooff, Mary Shaw, Betty Bench, Glynis Gunter, David Ryder, John Lester, Douglas Taylor, Patrick Rose, Luke Albarin.

The play was directed by Brian J. Burton
Settings designed by Tim Gowcher *and* David Perry
Stage Manager Trevor Beddoes
Lighting Chris Brazier
Costumes Shirley Goldfinch
Musical Director Noel Vine

CHARACTERS IN THE PLAY (*in order of appearance*)

Mrs Wilson, a good woman, in the vale of years
Mary Wilson, the sweet heroine
Squire Cribbs, a villain of the deepest dye
Edward Middleton, the hero with a lesson to learn
Sophia Spindle, an eccentric spinster
William Dowton, a simple rustic
Agnes Dowton, his poor demented sister
Mrs Miller, a villager of three score and ten summers
Mrs Gates, a villager with a taste for gossip
Mrs Stevens, another villager with a similar taste
Sam Adams, an elderly rustic with a thirst
The Landlord, of the village inn
Julia Middleton, an innocent child
Arden Rencelaw, a noble philanthropist
An Officer of the Law
Villagers, a Clergyman, etc.
(Non-speaking parts which may be omitted or increased)

ACT I
Scene 1   Interior of a pretty cottage in Hertfordshire towards the end of the 19th century.
Scene 2   A leafy lane in the village—later the same day.
Scene 3   Interior of Miss Spindle's house—some weeks later.
Scene 4   The leafy lane—two months later.
Scene 5   Exterior of the cottage—later the same day.

ACT II
Scene 1   Miss Spindle's house—a few weeks later.
Scene 2   The leafy lane—TEN YEARS LATER.
Scene 3   The village inn—TWO YEARS LATER.
Scene 4   The leafy lane—several months later.
Scene 5   Interior of the cottage—some weeks later.

ACT III
Scene 1   A street in London—TWO YEARS LATER.
Scene 2   A wretched garret in London—the next night.
Scene 3   The London street—early the next morning.
Scene 4   The same—the next day.
Scene 5   The exterior of the cottage in the village—later the same day.

The running time of the play is 2 hours 15 minutes including the songs but excluding intervals.

SONGS

ACT I

A Mother's Love (Mrs Wilson and Mary)
Now I've Found Thee (Edward and Mary)
I'm a Charmer (Miss Spindle)
Wedding Day (The Company)

ACT II

Old Devil Temptation (William)
He Has Fallen (Cribbs)
Those Who Are Good (Julia)

ACT III

Pity a Girl (Miss Spindle)
Though He Has Left Me (Mary and Julia)
Down with Demon Drink (Edward and the Landlord)
Those Who Are Good — *Reprise* (The Company)
Curtain Call Medley (The Company)

A full music plot appears at the end of the book and cues are given throughout the text.
The full piano score is available from Samuel French Ltd.

To

THE SWAN THEATRE COMPANY

INTRODUCTION

The 'delirium tremens dramas'—as they came to be known—had their roots in England probably as the result of a series of illustrations by George Cruikshank, the original illustrator of Dickens. These were published by the artist, who was himself an ardent teetotaller, under the title of *The Drunkard's Progress*. They were dramatised and performed with considerable success both in this country and in America, where the temperance movement was gathering strength.

The theme proved so popular in the theatre that the list of plays written and performed in the 19th century details scores of plays with titles such as *The Drunkard's Children*, *The Drunkard's Doom*, *The Drunkard's Glass*, *The Drunkard's Warning*, *The Drunkard's Sin*, *The Drunken Cobbler*, *The Drunken News-writer*, *The Drunken Recruit*, and so on.

Many of these plays crossed the Atlantic but soon the American writers started to turn out plays of their own on the same theme. The showman P. T. Barnum had taken over the Boston Museum and opened it as a miniature world fair. He was an energetic temperance lecturer and in the winter of 1844 presented, in the lecture hall of the Museum, the first production of *The Drunkard* or *The Fallen Saved*—'a moral domestic drama of American life in five acts'.

The authorship of the play is in some doubt, but it is certain that an American actor, William Henry Smith (1806-72), was a major contributor. He had been a hard drinker who had 'signed the pledge', and his experience both in this respect and in the theatre assured a considerable degree of authenticity.

The foreword of the first published edition of the play states that 'the proprietor of the Museum engaged a gentleman of known and appreciated literary requirements to undertake the task'. It would appear, however, that the result was not acceptable as written, for the foreword goes on to say that the play, 'though eminently worthy of the gentleman and the scholar was, from want of theatrical experience, merely a story in dialogue, entirely deficient in stage tact and dramatic effect'. So the script was 'placed in the hands of Wm. H. Smith with the request that he would finish it and prepare it for the stage'. This he did; the adaptation, under his own direction and with himself playing the hero, opened in Boston where it played for 130 nights. Its success was repeated later at another Barnum Museum, in New York.

It is not impossible that Barnum himself wrote the original text and that Smith, who was engaged to direct it and act the leading role, refused to do so unless he was allowed to do some rewriting. This would not have pleased the showman and could account for why the name of the 'gentleman' was never revealed. All this is mere speculation, but what is certain is that the play was a tremendous success and has survived together with William Pratt's *Ten Nights in a Bar Room* as one of the best-known of all temperance dramas.

Productions of *The Drunkard* have been numerous but perhaps its greatest viii The Drunkard

claim to fame is that, until recently, it held the world record for the longest run of any play. It opened at the Theatre Mart in Los Angeles on July 6th, 1933, and played every night without missing a single performance for twenty years, until September 6th, 1953. The following night *The Wayward Way*, a musical version of the same play, opened at the same theatre and played alternate nights with the straight version for another six years. It came off then only because the fire authorities condemned the theatre and it was forced to close. *The Wayward Way* was presented in this country at the New Lyric, Hammersmith, on November 16th, 1964, and transferred to the Vaudeville on January 27th, 1965.

In addition to the original American publication by Samuel French, New York, there have been editions published by Lacy, Dicks, and The Bodley Head. The last, published in 1943, was the 19th century adaptation by Thomas Hales Lacy, edited by Montagu Slater.

This new version is different from all the others in that it has been adapted to enable the action of the play to take place in England. This, of course, is not just a matter of altering the locations of the scenes. Furthermore, the dialogue has been trimmed in some places and expanded in others to make the speeches and situations stronger, and much of it has been rewritten. Whole scenes have been omitted and new ones substituted where it was felt that modern audiences would find them tiresome or too full of contemporary references. Minor characters have been 'axed' and others made to 'change their sex' so that the play can be more easily cast by modern drama groups with a preponderance of women. Ten original songs in the Victorian manner have been added, as those which were without doubt performed in the original version have been lost without trace. In spite of all these alterations, however, the intention has been to provide a melodrama with the same flavour as the original but with the same sort of appeal to modern audiences that the other plays in the series have enjoyed all over the world during the past few years.

However, the plot of *The Drunkard* is much nearer to conventional melodrama than the more sensational *Maria Marten* and *Sweeney Todd*, or even *Lady Audley's Secret* and *East Lynne*. All the basic ingredients are included. There is the pure and innocent heroine who, in spite of trial and tribulation, is ever faithful and forgiving. There is the utterly ruthless and despicable villain who is inevitably defeated in the end—in Victorian morality, the wages of sin must be death. The manly hero, although allowed to stray from the path of virtue, reforms, and is re-united with his long-suffering wife. There is the comic man who is not quite as simple as he seems at first sight and who always turns up in the nick of time, no matter how unlikely the locality, to rescue the hero or heroine in distress. We have the sweet wide-eyed child, usually with long flaxen hair, who seems preoccupied with thoughts of death and of Heaven and angels. There is the eccentric spinster (often this is a clergyman or some other professional man) for comic relief and the opportunity for poking gentle fun at the nobility or upper classes, and finally there is the 'heavy' who turns up late in the play like 'deus ex machina' to put things right and deliver a protracted homily.

Introduction

The play is full of rhetoric and one word is rarely used where a dozen can be employed. Oddly enough, although it is doubtful if the porter-swilling, gin-tippling audience understood one word of the verbose speeches, providing that they didn't occur too frequently they were every bit as popular and exciting as a good murder. Above all else, virtue was triumphant. It had to be; this was a strongly-held Victorian belief from which no melodramatist dared to deviate even had he wished to do so. If a present-day audience will accept this as truth for the duration of the performance they will be able to enter into it with the same artless and innocent pleasure as the audience of a hundred years ago most certainly did.

BRIAN J. BURTON

COPYRIGHT INFORMATION

(See also page ii)

This play is fully protected under the Copyright Laws of the British Commonwealth of Nations, the United States of America and all countries of the Berne and Universal Copyright Conventions.

All rights including Stage, Motion Picture, Radio, Television, Public Reading, and Translation into Foreign Languages, are strictly reserved.

No part of this publication may lawfully be reproduced in ANY form or by any means—photocopying, typescript, recording (including video-recording), manuscript, electronic, mechanical, or otherwise—or be transmitted or stored in a retrieval system, without prior permission.

Licences for amateur performances are issued subject to the understanding that it shall be made clear in all advertising matter that the audience will witness an amateur performance; that the names of the authors of the plays shall be included on all programmes; and that the integrity of the authors' work will be preserved.

The Royalty Fee is subject to contract and subject to variation at the sole discretion of Samuel French Ltd.

In Theatres or Halls seating Six Hundred or more the fee will be subject to negotiation.

In Territories Overseas the fee quoted above may not apply. A fee will be quoted on application to our local authorized agent, or if there is no such agent, on application to Samuel French Ltd, London.

VIDEO RECORDING OF AMATEUR PRODUCTIONS

Please note that the copyright laws governing the video-recording are extremely complex and that it should not be assumed that any play may be video-recorded for whatever purpose without first obtaining the permission of the appropriate agents. The fact that a play is published by Samuel French Ltd does not indicate that video rights are available or that Samuel French Ltd controls such rights.

Music 1: Overture

ACT I

SCENE 1

The interior of a pretty cottage in a village in Hertfordshire about thirty miles from London

The year is 1880 (or any other year in the 19th century in which you may decide to set the play)

The setting of this scene (in common with all the others in the play) is as simple as possible. Only the bare essentials of furniture and stage properties are used. All entrances, throughout the play, are either from left or right. Full-stage settings alternate with front stage scenes to enable the simple changes to be made

The setting of this scene consists of a backing set against back traverse curtains. On this backing is painted a window and the view through it as well as the curtains and pictures, etc. (See Production Notes at end of book)

There is a table left centre stage on which is a family bible and an aspidistra. There are chairs to the right and left of the table and an armchair DRC. Mrs Wilson, a woman in her late sixties, is seated in the armchair and her daughter Mary is seated left of the table working at an embroidery frame

Music 2: Heroine Theme 'A' (softly)

Mrs Wilson (*breathing a deep sigh*) Ah me, what is to become of us?
Mary Hush, Mother! Do not distress yourself so.
Mrs Wilson How can I fail to do so? It was here in this very room that your poor, dear father breathed his last. This very chair is indeed dear to me for it was in this he sat the very day before he left the cares of this mortal world behind him for ever.
Mary Dear, dear Father.
Mrs Wilson (*rising and moving US of table*) Oh, how he loved this calm retreat, this dear cottage which has been our happy home for so many years of bliss. Many times, during his last terrible illness, he rejoiced that when her earthly days were o'er, the dear companion of his years would close her eyes in these rural shades and be laid in yon little nook beside him, (*she sighs and sits in the armchair R*) but now . . .

Music 2 ends

2 The Drunkard

Mary (*putting her embroidery on the table*) Dear Mother, 'tis true. This sweet cottage is most dear to us, but we are but the tenants. Our worthy landlord, old Mr Middleton troubled us but little, but now he is no more. It is rumoured abroad that our little home is to be sold. But we cannot censure his son for that.

Mrs Wilson No; the young must be provided for. For my own part, I willingly would bow with resignation to Heaven which loveth while it chasteneth. But when I think that you, my beloved, my only child, will be exposed to the thousand temptations of life as a penniless orphan, then I begin to fear that ...

There is a knock, off L

Hark! (*She rises*) What was that?

There is another knock

Ah, a knock! (*Calling*) Who is it? (*To Mary*) Dry your tears, my darling. We must not let our visitor observe us weeping. (*Calling*) Come in.

Music 3: Villain Theme (briefly)

Squire Cribbs enters L. He is a man in his sixties, dressed in the traditional costume of the villains of melodrama

Mrs Wilson Good morning, sir. Mary, my child, a chair for the Squire.

Mary moves her chair DL for the Squire and crosses to in front of the table. Mrs Wilson sits in the armchair

Cribbs Good morning, Mrs Wilson. Good morning, my dear young lady.

Mary curtsies and then sits in the chair right of the table

Mary Good morning, sir.
Cribbs (*sitting*) No doubt you have heard the dreadful news.
Mrs Wilson Indeed yes.
Cribbs 'Tis a sad calamity that has befallen the village, my good Mrs Wilson.
Mrs Wilson There's many a poor person, I fear, will have reason to think so, sir.
Cribbs You are right. He was a good man, that Mr Middleton. Many's the time he came to me for the benefit of my legal advice. He placed great confidence in it. I am proud to have been of service to him. He was my very dear friend.
Mary It is rumoured that he was very rich at one time, Mr Cribbs.
Cribbs 'Tis true—when the times were good. But bad speculations, unlucky investments, false friends accounted for every penny that he had. (*Rising*) He died without a halfpenny to pass on to his son. Alas, alas! We all have our ups and downs, my dear madam.
Mrs Wilson Ah, Squire, I perceive you are a man, who——
Cribbs Has a heart to feel for the unfortunate. True, true, madam. It is

Act I, Scene 1

the character I have attained, though far be it from me to boast. Now, the main reason for my visit is to enquire about your future welfare.

Mrs Wilson You are most kind, Squire.

Cribbs Not at all—not at all. (*Moving DS slightly; aside*) Little does she know the true purpose of my visit. Ha! Ha! (*Aloud*) Tell me, my dear Mrs Wilson, have you any prospect of—that is to say—have you provided—

Mary (*rising and moving DS*) It is true then—too true. The cottage and the garden will be sold?

Cribbs Why, what can the young man do, my dear? A giddy young man like him—fond of the world and given somewhat to excess, and without any sort of inheritance from his late lamented father. (*Moving L of Mary*) But pardon me, my dear Miss Mary, I would not call up a blush on the cheek of modesty. But you know, the extravagance, that is the folly—

Mrs Wilson Alas, sir, yes. I would say he is very much unlike his poor, dear departed father.

Cribbs Do not misunderstand me. I wish the young man well, with all my heart. Heaven knows I have cause to do so for his honoured father's sake. (*He brings out a handkerchief and puts it to his eyes with a great deal of show*)

Mrs Wilson Come, come, Mr Cribbs. He is better off. We must not mourn the death of a good man. It would be impiety. His end was that of a Christian!

Cribbs (*blowing his nose violently*) You are right, Mrs Wilson. Judge then of the interest which I take in the last remaining scion of that honoured stock. (*Aside*) 'Tis fortunate she does not know the true reason for my interest. (*Aloud*) But, madam, Edward Middleton—he is yet young and—

Mrs Wilson He cannot be more than twenty. I recollect him when a lad—a bright, blue-eyed boy with flaxen hair, tall for his age.

Cribbs Twenty-three last July, madam; that is his age to the day. But he is giddy, wild and reckless. (*A pause. He looks round the room, and moves to front of chair L.*) Well, madam, business is business. I am a plain man, Mrs Wilson, and sometimes called too blunt—and—

Mary Then we must leave the cottage, sir?

Cribbs (*pretending feeling*) No—no—not *yet*, my dear young lady. But it might be best to be prepared. Edward is inclined to be impulsive and once he has made up his mind, no power in Heaven or earth would change him from his course. I know that if I were to go down before him on bended knees, all my entreaties on your behalf would be of no avail. It might be prudent to look around for another place before he moves in the matter. It might save you from much inconvenience.

Mrs Wilson You impose upon us a severe task, my dear sir.

Cribbs Bear up, my dear madam—bear up. If I may be so officious, I would suggest that you try Hitchin. (*He moves to L of Mary*) Any healthy young woman, like your daughter, can obtain a profitable situation there. Think of it, my good madam. I will see you again before very long. (*He moves to exit L and turns*) And now Heaven bless you.

4   The Drunkard

Mary (*moving to Mrs Wilson*) Mother, Mother—what is to become of us?
Mrs Wilson (*rising and putting her arm round Mary*) My child, my poor,
poor child.

Music 4: Villain Theme

Cribbs (*by the exit; aside*) Well—that interview of mock sympathy and
charity is over, and I flatter myself pretty well acted too. Ha! Ha! Yes,
the widow and her child must quit the cottage—I'm resolved. First for
the wrongs I years ago endured from old Mr Wilson and secondly, it
suits my own interests—and this is what matters above all other con-
siderations. Now for the next stage in my plot. I will seek out young
Middleton and give him the benefit of my 'advice'. Ha! Ha! Ha!

Squire Cribbs exits L and Music 4 ends

Mrs Wilson Comfort, my daughter. It is a good thing to have a friend in
the hour of trouble. This Mr Cribbs appears to be a very feeling man.
Nevertheless, before we take his advice, we would do well to make our
proposed trial of this young man, Edward Middleton. Are you ready?
Mary Yes, Mother.
Mrs Wilson You have the money in your purse?
Mary It is all here, Mother. Thirty crowns—the sum we have saved to
purchase fuel for the winter.
Mrs Wilson That will pay off part of the amount owing for rent. When
this young man finds we are disposed to deal fairly with him, he may
relent. You turn pale, Mary. What ails you, child?
Mary Dear Mother—'Tis nothing. It will soon be over. It must be done,
but I fear this young man. He has a reputation for being wild and
reckless.
Mrs Wilson Fear not, Mary—fear not. Remember what I have told you.
Call him to the door. Do not enter the house—just give him the money,
and tell him your sad story. He must, from family and association at
least, have the manners of a gentleman—and however wild a youth may
be, when abroad among his associates, no gentleman ever insulted a
friendless and unprotected woman!

Music 5: Chords (briefly)

Mary You give me courage, dear Mother. (*Aside*) I tremble at the thought
of what I needs must do. (*She goes to exit L*) Goodbye, dear Mother.

The introduction to Music 6 begins

Mrs Wilson Go forth, my child—go as the dove flew from the ark of old,
and if thou shouldst fail in finding the olive branch of peace, return, and
seek comfort where thou shalt surely find it—in the bosom of thy fond
and widowed mother.

Act I, Scene 1

Music 6: A Mother's Love

Verse

Mrs Wilson
>When you are lonely, when you are sad,
>When times are trying, when times are bad,
>There is a haven where you may rest —
>Safe and contented on your mother's breast.

Mary crosses to L of Mrs Wilson who puts her arm on Mary's shoulder

Mrs Wilson } *(together)*
Mary
>A mother's love will never fade.
>A mother's love is true.
>And you need never be afraid
>For she will comfort you.

Mary breaks away to C stage

Mary When I am lonely, when I am sad,
>When times are trying, when times are bad,
>There is a haven where I may rest —
>Safe and contented on my mother's breast.

Mrs Wilson to R of Mary — heads close together for final chorus

Mrs Wilson } *(together)*
Mary
>A mother's love will never fade.
>A mother's love is true.
>And you need never be afraid
>For she will comfort you.

At the end of the song Mary moves to exit L

6   The Drunkard

Mary I go, Mother. I go.

Mrs Wilson God be with you on your mission, my child! God be with you!

Music 7: A Mother's Love into Heroine Theme B

Fade to Black-out

SCENE 2

A leafy lane in the village—later the same day

This is a front stage scene played against either a painted drop cloth or traverse curtains. There is a low cut-out tree profile stage right set far enough forward to enable characters to hide behind it

Mary enters R

Mary I have almost reached the residence of Mr Edward Middleton. In a few minutes, I shall see this dissipated young man. Oh, my poor mother must be deceived! How can a man such as he have pity for the children of poverty? (*Moving towards the tree*) We are but misfortune's suppliants for shelter beneath the roof of his cottage ... but who is this who approaches? 'Tis a gentleman. My fears tell me that he is the man I seek. Shall I ever have the courage to speak? I will pause till he has reached the house. (*She hides behind the tree*)

Music 7 ends

Music 8: Villain Theme (briefly)

Cribbs enters left. Edward Middleton enters right and crosses to centre. They meet CS

Cribbs Good day, son of my old friend! I have been looking for you.

Edward (*shaking hands*) Mr Cribbs, your most obedient servant. You may be sure that any friend of my father is more than welcome.

Cribbs Well said—nobly said. I see your father before me, when I look on you.

Edward And what may I have the pleasure of doing for you, Mr Cribbs?

Cribbs But a trifling matter, Mr Middleton. So trivial that I hesitate to bother you with it. Nevertheless, as your late father's legal adviser, I am obliged to do so.

Edward Yes?

Cribbs It is with regard to the cottage and the lands adjoining. When last we talked upon the subject—

Mary peeps L of the tree

Edward I was then ignorant that a poor widow and her only child—

Act I, Scene 2   7

Cribbs Who are in arrears for rent—

Edward Had lived there for many years, and that my father esteemed them most highly.

Cribbs That may be so, but you must not allow your heart to rule your head, young man. That is a fatal mistake that has led many a foolish man along the pathway that leads to ruin.

Edward (*turning and moving R slightly*) I could not turn them forth upon the world in the present condition of the old lady. She is ailing and may not be much longer for this world.

Cribbs Have you not heard of the workhouse?

Edward turns to Cribbs. Mary bobs up from behind the tree

Music 9: Chords

Edward The workhouse, Mr Cribbs? Certainly not! They must stay in the cottage that has been their home. How could I send them forth from the flowers which they have reared, the vines which they have trained in their course—a place endeared to them by tender domestic recollections and past remembrances of purity and happiness?

Cribbs What of the fences which they have neglected—the garden gate which is off its hinges—the branches of the old birch tree broken down for firewood—eh?

Edward (*moving to C raising his hand in protest*) Enough, Mr Cribbs, enough! I will not listen to you further. All this has been explained to me by my foster brother, William. The trees and the fences were broken down by idle school boys.

Cribbs (*crossing to Edward*) On reflection, I believe that I now understand you better. I comprehend your plan. We are both men of the world, are we not?

Edward I fail to understand you, sir.

Cribbs Well—the daughter—a fine girl, eh? Sparkling eyes, eh? (*Digging Edward in the ribs*) Dimples, eh? Roguish glances, eh? Ah, when I was young, eh? Ah, well—never mind. You have seen her, eh?

Edward I have never seen the girl. Explain yourself, Mr Cribbs.

Cribbs If you have not seen her—you will, eh? I understand. (*He takes a quick glance off stage L*) Little presents of game from the estate—mother and daughter grateful—eh? Eh? Very grateful—free access to the cottage at all hours, eh?

Edward Cribbs, you do not—you cannot mean what I—

Cribbs Why not? Why not?

Edward Cribbs—do you know that this girl has no father?

Cribbs Exactly—exactly. A very wild flower growing on the open heath.

Edward Have you forgotten that this poor girl has not a brother?

Cribbs That's it! A garden without a fence—not a stake standing. You have nothing to do but—step inside. Ha! Ha!

Edward (*catching hold of Cribbs by his lapels*) You villain, you cad, you cur! I respect your grey hairs. That is fortunate for you. (*He looses hold,*

8   The Drunkard

pushes Cribbs away and takes a pace backwards) But I knew an old man once—peace to his ashes—whose hair was as grey as yours. Beneath that aged breast there beat a heart as pure as the first throbs of childhood. I let you go in peace. But had that old man heard you utter such foul sentences to his son; had he heard you tell me to enter, like a wolf, this fold of innocence, and tear from her mother's arms the hope of her old age, he would have forgotten the winters that had dried the pith within his aged limbs, seized you by the throat, and dashed you prostrate to the earth, as too foul a carcass to walk erect and mock the name of man.

Cribbs I perceive you are put out.

Edward (*moving away R*) Leave me, old man; begone! Your hot, lascivious breath cannot mingle with the sweet perfume of these wild flowers. Your raven voice will not harmonize with the warblings of these heavenly song birds which pour forth their praises to that Almighty Power, who looks with horror on your brutal crime. Begone! (*He points off L*)

Mary rushes to Edward and kneels at his feet

Mary The blessings of the widowed and fatherless be upon thee. May they accompany thy voice to Heaven's tribunal, not to cry for vengeance, but to plead for pardon for this wicked man.

Cribbs (*aside*) Ha! The widow's daughter. Now I must practice some artifice. (*Aloud*) Mr Middleton, you mistake me. I was but suggesting that you might visit these dear people to give them the benefit of your manly protection.

Mary weeps

I cannot endure a woman's tears. Poor, poor child. May heaven bless thee and protect thee. (*He moves towards the exit L*)

Music 10: Villain Theme (briefly)

(*Aside*) I'll be terribly revenged for this.

Cribbs exits

Edward (*aside*) This, then, is the widow's child. (*Aloud, turning to Mary and placing his hand on her head*) Rise, my dear and be assured of my sympathy for your mother's sorrows and of my assistance in your hour of need.

Mary (*rising*) Thank you, sir, for your cheering kindness. But I have an errand for you. (*Holding out her purse*) This is part of the rent which——

Edward Nay, then, you have not overheard my discourse with the old man, who has just left us. I have told him——

Music 11: Heroine Theme A (softly)

Mary Sir, I cannot tell a lie. I overheard all. We are to remain in the cottage. Oh, sir, is that any reason to withhold from you your due? It is

Act I, Scene 2

now paid with double pleasure, since we recognize a benefactor in our creditor. Take this, I entreat—'tis but a portion of the debt, but be assured, the remainder shall be paid as soon as busy, willing hands can earn it.

Edward (*aside; moving DL*) This young girl has quite taken my breath away. She is the most charming, most delightful, most beautiful girl that I have ever had the good fortune to behold.

Music 11 ends

(*Aloud; turning to Mary*) Nay, nay, dear girl, I do not require your money. Be pleased to retain it as a portion of your dowry.

Mary Sir!

Edward If, as you say, you overheard the conversation that I just held with that old man, you must know that I sometimes speak very plainly.

Mary (*apprehensively*) Yes, sir. Alas, it is not our fault that the fences are broken down. When my poor father lived, it was not so. But since——

Edward When that vile old man spoke to me of your charms, I heeded him not. There are plenty of pretty girls in this part of Hertfordshire, but I have now discovered for myself what I had heard before—something more than ordinary beauty—a charm of mental excellence, noble sentiment, filial piety. These are the beauties that render you conspicuous above all the maidens I have ever seen. (*Moving to Mary*) I speak plainly, for I speak honestly, and when I ask you to keep that money as a portion of your dowry, need I say into whose hands I would like it to fall at last?

Mary (*with bowed head*) To affect—to affect not to understand you, sir, would be an idle return for kindness such as yours, and yet——

Edward I sometimes walk down in the vicinity of your cottage, and——

Mary Should I see you go by without stopping—why then—why then——

Edward Then what—dear, dear Mary?

Mary Then should I suppose you had forgotten where we lived.

Edward Mary, my dearest—how could I ever forget? (*Aside*) Ah, little did I think when I contemplated selling that dear cottage, that it should be regarded as a casket, invaluable for the jewel it contained. (*Aloud; turning to Mary*) Mary, my dear, I have spoken plainly. Now will I venture even further. (*He takes a step towards Mary*) Will you—(*another step*)—could you?

Mary Oh, Edward!

Edward Would you do me the great honour of becoming my wife?

Mary But, Edward, I have but met you these few moments.

Edward In reality, but a few moments, but in my dreams have I known you all my life.

The introduction to Music 12 plays slowly

Marry me, Mary, and we will make your cottage our home, and my foster brother and his poor demented sister shall live on in mine.

Mary You overwhelm me, sir. What can I say?

Edward Say yes, say yes!

Music 12: Now I've Found Thee

Edward Now I've found thee, dearest heart
I will love thee ever,
And I vow we'll never part.
Nothing will us sever.

Mary (*turning away*)
But I scarcely know thee, sir.
Thou art nigh a stranger,
And I fear I must demur.
I might be in danger.

Edward (*to Mary, placing his hand on her shoulder*)
Oh, my love, thou must not fear.
Thou canst ever trust me.
Thou art safe with me, my dear.
I would never harm thee.

Mary (*turning to Edward*)
I believe thee, dearest love
Though I've lately met thee,
And I pray to Heaven above
Thou wilt ever love me.

Edward
Mary } (*together, holding their hands outstretched*)
Now I've found thee, dearest heart
I will love thee ever,
And I vow we'll never part.
Nothing will us sever.

Act I, Scene 3   11

They embrace

> And I vow we'll never part.
> Nothing will us sever.

Mary Very well, Edward, I consent. I will marry you.
Edward My dear, dear Mary.

The lights fade to Black-out

Music 13: Now I've Found Thee into chorus of **I'm A Charmer**

Music 13 ends as Scene 3 commences

SCENE 3

The interior of Miss Spindle's house—some weeks later

This is a full stage setting played against the back traverse curtains. There is a table set at a slight angle centre stage with a chair above it. The table is covered with toilet articles and there is a small standing mirror on it facing upstage. There is a chair DL of the table and an armchair DR. Miss Spindle, a spinster of advanced years, dressed in the clothes of a young woman, is seated behind the table. She speaks in a "refained" voice but is rather uncertain of her Hs

Miss Spindle The attractions of the fair sex are synonymous. Alas, 'tis true that Father Time is the destroyer of female charms, but as my favourite poet says—"Age cannot wither me, nor custom stale my infinite vacuity". But time is money, so money must be time. Thus we bring back, by the aid of money, the times of youth. I value my beauty at fifty crowns a year, as that is about the amount it costs me to keep it in repair. I have heard it said that a pair of boots when soled and heeled, are better than when they were new. Why should it not be so with our charms? We can have red cheeks at seventy, and thanks to the artistry of the dentist, good teeth at any time of life. (*She rises and moves DR*) Woman was made for love. They suppose that my heart is not susceptible of the tender passion. But the heart can be regulated by money, too. I buy all the affecting novels and all the terrible romances, and read them till my heart has become soft as maiden wax, to receive the impression of that cherished image I adore. (*She looks towards the window*) Ah—if my eyes don't deceive me—there goes his foster brother, William, by my window. (*She goes to the window and calls*) Hem! Hem! William! Wil-li-am!
William (*off*) Good day to 'ee, Miss Spindle.
Miss Spindle Come on inside for a moment, William.
William (*off*) Thank 'ee kindly, Miss Spindle, but I be——
Miss Spindle Tut, tut, William! You naughty boy, are you trying to avoid me? I won't take no for an answer. I'll not detain you long.

12   The Drunkard

William (*off*) Oh, very well then but I musn't stop.

Miss Spindle returns to table and sits and primps at the mirror

William enters slowly left holding his hat in his hands, twisting it. He carries a bag of nuts

Miss Spindle Come along in, then, William—take a chair.

William moves in front of the chair L

There's no need to be shy. You're far too modest, I declare.

William I be fair modest, and that's a fact. (*He sits awkwardly in the chair*) I'll tell 'ee, I be that modest, I allus goes to bed without a candle.

Miss Spindle Would you like me to tell you what I have thought, William?

William If 'ee's a mind to, Miss. I don't care much about it one way or t'other, if 'ee wants to know. (*He rises and offers Miss Spindle a paper bag*) Would 'ee like a nut?

Miss Spindle You are very kind, but I must decline your generous offer.

William (*shrugging his shoulders and returning to his chair*) Just as 'ee pleases. T'aint no skin off my nose, and that's a fact.

Miss Spindle This is what I have thought. There are two sorts of men. Do you know what I mean?

William Aye, that I do. There be tall ones and short ones, like cigars. (*With exaggerated illustration*)

Miss Spindle You mistake my meaning, William.

William (*scratching his head*) Ah, now what can 'ee mean then? Two sorts of men? I got it—fat ones and thin ones!

Miss Spindle No, William—no!

William Black ones and white ones?

Miss Spindle (*rising; moving away R*) No, William. What I mean is, that some are warm and susceptible to the charms of women while others are cold and apparently insensible to our beauties. (*Turning to William*). Do you follow me?

William (*blankly*) Why, where be 'ee going?

Miss Spindle I'm not going anywhere, William. What I am trying to say is that I have a confession I would confide in your generous secrecy. I have a trembling affection——

William (*rising*) Oh, dear—that sounds awful bad. (*Moving to L of Miss Spindle*) Has 'ee seen a doctor?

Miss Spindle It's not a doctor I need, William. There is a warm, yet modest flame——

William (*aside*) Trembling infection, warm flame! I reckon the old girl's got the ague.

Miss Spindle Tell me, dear William, how can I combat with this dear, yet relentless, foe?

William Well, I reckons if 'ee puts thy feet in a hot mustard bath, and covers thyself with thick blankets 'ee'll be as right as ninepence, in the morning.

Miss Spindle William! (*She moves away and sits in the armchair*)

Act I, Scene 3   13

William Well, that be old Mrs Brown's recipe for fever and ague, and it ain't never been known to fail—I tell 'ee.

Miss Spindle You mistake me, William. I have an ardent passion.

William (*moving one step towards Miss Spindle*) Ooh—'ee mustn't get into a passion, Miss Spindle. It be awful bad for thy ague and fever.

Miss Spindle You will not understand! I have a passion for one——

William It be a good thing it be only for one or 'ee——

Miss Spindle Can you not fancy who that one is?

William (*scratching his head*) Danged if I can.

Miss Spindle He lives in your house.

William In my house? Now then—there be I—I lives there, and Mr Middleton, and my poor little sister Agnes. Now then—it ain't Agnes as her is a woman, so then it must be—why, it be I or Mr Middleton. (*Laughing*) See I worked that out all right.

Miss Spindle I fear, dear William, that I must tell you that you are not the object of my affection.

William (*aside*) What a relief. She had I proper worried for a minute. (*Aloud*) I see. Then I reckons if it not be I—then it must be Mr Middleton!

Miss Spindle Mr Middleton indeed—Mr Edward Middleton (*She sighs*)

William (*aside*) Dang me if her ain't setting her cap at my foster brother. I reckons as how I'd better get her talking on summat else. (*Aloud, moving to L of Miss Spindle*) That be a grand pink dress you be wearing, Miss Spindle. It becomes 'ee.

Miss Spindle (*affecting coyness*) You shouldn't say things like that, Mr William.

William Right you be, Miss Spindle. I'll not say nothing no more. (*He turns away*)

Miss Spindle (*disappointed*) Oh—er. How does it become me?

William (*turning back*) It matches very well indeed, Miss Spindle.

Miss Spindle Matches with what, William?

William Why, with thy eyes.

Miss Spindle (*with obvious displeasure*) Yes! Now, William, how about the cottage? When are you going to turn out those Wilsons?

William Don't 'ee worry, Miss Spindle. There be someone else going to live there and afore very long. (*Aside*) Little does her know it be my foster brother, Edward.

Miss Spindle (*rising*) I'm glad to hear it. I never could endure those Wilsons. I know they haven't paid their rent, and do you know that girl was seen getting into a chaise with a young man, and didn't return until nine at night. It was too dark to see who the young man was, even though I stood there in the rain for hours waiting for them to come back.

William Ah, that explains it, Miss Spindle.

Miss Spindle Explains what?

William How 'ee caught that ague and fever 'ee was on about—getting soaked in all that rain. (*Moving L*) Well, good day to 'ee, Miss Spindle.

Miss Spindle (*following him*) You're leaving me?

William (*turning back*) That I be, but afore I go, let I give 'ee a bit of advice. 'Ee must take good care of thy precious health, Miss Spindle. Keep thy feet warm, and thy head cool, and thy mouth shut, and thy heart open, and, very soon, I reckon 'ee'll have good health, good conscience, and stand well on thy pins. Good day to 'ee.
Miss Spindle Well, really!

William exits L

Miss Spindle The vulgar creature! He ought to know that English ladies don't have "pins". But for all this, I am certain that my dear, dear Edward is dying for me. As the poet says "He lets concealment, like a worm in the bud feed on the damask curtains of ... his ... cheek ..." or is it "damask bud"? I'm sure there's a bud in it somewhere.

The introduction to Music 14 starts

No matter, of one thing I'm certain—my charms are as yet undecayed.

Music 14: I'm a Charmer

Chorus (C)   I'm a charmer, a disarmer
And the men all fall, you see.
I'm angelic—and sirenic.
It's no wonder they love me.

Verse (to DL)   If you look through all the pages
Of the books of history,
You will find, throughout the ages,
Famous beauties just like me.

Chorus (C)   I'm a charmer—a disarmer
And the men all fall, you see.
A beguiler—a Delilah.
It's no wonder they love me.

Act I, Scene 3   15

She moves to the chair behind the table, sits and looks in the mirror

Verse Though I'm modest and retiring
There's one thing I can't deny,
If a beauty you're desiring
No one is more fair than I.

Chorus I'm a charmer, a disarmer
And the men all fall, you see.
I'm a teaser—Mona Lisa.
It's no wonder they love me.

Verse (*rising; to C*) Can I help it if I'm charming,
An exquisite cynosure?
There are times it's quite alarming
When the men flock at my door.

Chorus I'm a charmer, a disarmer
And the men all fall you see
I'm a flighty—Aphrodite.
It's no wonder they love me.
No wonder they-love-me.

And even when old age *does* come on, the charm of refined education
will still remain. As the poet says:
You may break, you may ruin the vase if you will,
The scent of the roses will cling round it still.

The lights fade to Black-out

Music 15: I'm Charmer into Villain Theme

SCENE 4

The leafy lane—two months later

Cribbs enters R

Music 16: Villain Theme

Cribbs (*to audience*) So, Mary Wilson is to marry Edward Middleton this
very day. Thus ends my prudent endeavours to get rid of the Wilsons.
But, young Middleton—there is yet some hope of him. I will do him
some unexpected favour, worm myself into his good graces. Then I will
invite him into the bar of the village inn, and if he falls—Ha! Ha! Ha!
I shall see them begging their bread yet; the wife on her bended knees
to me, praying for a morsel of food for her starving children.

16 The Drunkard

Music 16 ends

That will be revenge—revenge indeed! (*He moves DR and faces L*) Ha! Ha! But who is this approaching? Ah, 'tis his foster brother, Simple William. I'll wheedle him—try the ground before I put my foot upon it.

William enters left, whistling. He moves C

William Ah, Squire Cribbs! Has 'ee seen my poor little, half-witted sister, Agnes?

Cribbs (*moving towards William*) No, William, my honest fellow, I have not. (*Aside; moving DS slightly*) Nor want to, I vow. She knows too much for my liking, although I am safe enough now that she has gone mad. Ha! Ha! (*Aloud*) But I want to speak to you for a moment.

William (*aside*) What be old razor chops awanting with I, I wonder. (*Aloud*) Well, Squire, what can I do for 'ee? I be in a terrible hurry.

Cribbs They keep you busy, eh?

William That they do. Has 'ee not heard? Mr Edward be getting wed this very day. (*Aside*) That be a regular dose for the Squire, I reckons—worse than senna and salts.

Cribbs Yes, yes, I had heard. (*With an artificial smile*) Delighted at the news! Delighted!

William I thought 'ee seemed pleased. (*Aside*) I reckons the old Squire looks as how he'd swallowed vinegar in mistake for cider.

Cribbs Give my best respects to Mr Edward.

William That I will, Squire. (*He starts to exit R*)

Cribbs Wait!

William checks and turns to Cribbs

There is one further matter I wish to discuss with you.

William Sir?

Cribbs You are a clever fellow, William. Now, can you show me just how clever you are by getting me an invitation to the wedding? Mr Edward and I had a slight difference of opinion, over a trifling matter, some months ago, but I am not one to bear a grudge. The wedding would seem an admirable opportunity to bury the hatchet with the son of my old and very dear friend. (*He moves L of William*) See what you can do in the matter of the invitation, and here's a crown to drink my health.

William Thank 'ee kindly, Squire, but I don't want none of thy money.

Cribbs Oh, very well—no offence meant, you know. Come now, let's step into the inn together, eh? And we'll drink the health of the young couple, eh?

William Squire Cribbs, it be my opinion that when your uncle Beelzebub wants to bribe an honest fellow to do a bad action, he'd better hire a pettifogging bad lawyer to tempt him, with a dud crown in one hand, and a bottle of whisky in t'other. Good day to 'ee.

William exits R

Cribbs (*looking after William*) Ah, Ah! For all your apparent stupidity, I

Act I, Scene 4

perceive you are a cunning scoundrel. But I'll fix you yet. Just you wait and see, my lad. But who is this approaching? Why it's his insane sister. She knows too much for my happiness. Will the creature never die? Her voice haunts me like the spectre of the youth that was engaged to her whom, for my own purposes I ruined. I triumphed over him. *(He moves US)* Ha! Ha! Ha! He could not resist the temptation—he fell the victim of drink. He died in a drunken fit and this wretched girl was driven insane. Ha! Ha! Ha!

Music 17: Agnes Theme

Agnes enters R. She is chanting. She moves about the stage scattering imaginary flowers

Agnes
Brake and fern and cypress dell,
Where the slippery adder crawls,
Where the grassy waters well,
By the old moss-covered walls
Upon the heather, when the weather
Is as wild as May,
So they prance as they dance,
And we'll all be gay.

Music 17 ends

But they poured too much red water in his glass. The lawyer is a fine man. Ha! Ha! Ha! He lives in the big house yonder. But the will—ah, ah,—the will——

Cribbs *(turning to Agnes)* Go home, Agnes—go home!

Agnes Home! *(She runs to the tree and kneels)* I saw a little wren yesterday. I had passed her nest often. I had counted the eggs. They were so pretty, so beautiful. *(She rises and moves R)* Rough Robin of the mill came this morning and stole them. The little bird went to her nest, and looked in—they were gone. She chirruped mournfully and flew away. *(She turns to face Cribbs)* She won't go home any more.

Cribbs *(crossing to Agnes)* Agnes, who let you out? You distress the whole village with your muttering and singing. *(Threatening her)* I'll have you taken care of!

Agnes *(slipping past him)* Did you know—there's to be a wedding in the village? *(Turning to face Cribbs)* I saw the coffin full of wedding cake.
        "And the bride was red with weeping.
        Cypress in her hair"
Can you tell me why they weep at weddings? Is it for joy? I used to weep when I was joyful—you never weep, old man. I should have been married, but my wedding dress was all covered with mildew, so we put off the wedding till another day. They'll make a new dress for me. They say I am mad and he won't come again. Am I mad? Am I? But the will—ha! ha! ha!—the will, old man—the will—ha! ha! ha!

18   The Drunkard

Cribbs (*crossing to Agnes*) Ah! Confusion! Get you gone, or thus I'll—(*He seizes her and raises his cane as if to hit her*)

Music 18: Villain Theme (fast)

William enters quickly R

William catches hold of Cribbs and throws him to the ground, and puts his foot on him

Music 18 ends

William Why 'ee black varmint! Strike my little, helpless half-crazed sister, would 'ee? If it were not for thy grey hairs, I'd break every bone in thy black beetle body.
Cribbs You'll live to regret this day, young man, if there's a law in this land. A plain case of assault and battery. (*Rising*) I'll have you in prison—I'll put you behind bars.

Cribbs exits R

Music 19: Villain Theme (on Cribb's exit)

William (*to Cribb's back*) I'll put 'ee in the duck pond if I sees 'ee touching my sister again, I promise 'ee.

William exits R

Agnes (*scattering imaginary flowers and chanting; moving C*)
        They lived down in the valley,
        Their house was painted red,
        And every day the robin came
        To pick the crumbs of bread.
But the grass does not wither when they die. I will stay here till I hear the bells that are far off, for then I think of his words. Who says he did not love me? It was a good character he wanted of the parson. A girl out of place, is like an old man out of his grave.

Music 20: Bells followed by Agnes Theme

They won't ask me to their merry-makings now, though I washed my best dress in the stream. Stream! Stream! Stream! (*Rushing to DSR and kneeling over an imaginary body and screaming*) Water! Water! Hear him—oh, hear him cry for water! Quick—he'll turn cold again! His lips are blue! (*Rising*) Water! Water!

Agnes exits R

The Lights fade to Black-out

Music 21: Bells into Wedding Day (continuing until Music 22)

Act I, Scene 5

19

SCENE 5

The exterior of the cottage—later the same day

This is a full stage setting with a backing of either a cyclorama or a painted backcloth. There is a cut-out cottage UL with a practical door. There is a tree RC with a bench in front of it, and another bench left of the cottage door

At the opening of the scene, villagers enter from left and right, and stand in groups. There is a great deal of excited chatter, anticipating the arrival of the bridal procession

Music 22: Wedding Day

All   Ding dong, ding dong,
What a very merry time.
Ding dong, ding dong,
Hear the wedding bells all chime.

Villager (*looking off UR*): They be coming!

Edward and Mary enter, UR, arm in arm during the second verse, followed by two bridesmaids, the Clergyman, Mrs Wilson and Mrs Miller

Edward and Mary move C, the Clergyman to LC Mrs Wilson to L of Clergyman and Mrs Miller to RC. The Bridesmaids part and stand one on each side of the Bride and Groom. The other Villagers are L or R

All   Ding dong, ding dong,
What a happy bride and groom,
Ding dong, ding dong,
Starting on their honeymoon.

During this verse the Clergyman comes behind and then between Edward and Mary, holding their hands. At the end of the verse he goes back to his original position. The Bridesmaid R goes to Mrs Miller who admires her dress

20   The Drunkard

All   Ding dong, ding dong,
                             Now their married life's begun,
                             Ding dong, ding dong,
                             For the parson's made them one.

William enters UR

William goes to right Bridesmaid and kisses her. She pushes him away DR

All   Ding dong, ding dong,
                             May their lives be full of joy.
                             Ding dong, ding dong,
                             First a girl and then a boy.

                             Ding dong, ding dong,
                             We all wish them well today,
                             Ding dong, ding dong,
                             On their happy wedding day.
                             On their wedding day.

Edward Dearest Mary—ah, indeed you are now my very own. Words are too poor, too weak to express the joy, the happiness that agitates my heart!

Music 23: Heroine Theme "A"

Ah, dear, dear wife—may each propitious day that dawns upon thy future life but add another flower to the rosy garland that now encircles thee!

Mary Thank you, Edward, my own beloved husband. Thy benison is echoed from my innermost heart.

Mrs Miller (*moving towards the bridal couple*) My dear Mary, your happiness sheds its genial rays around old and young. (*To Edward*) Young man, I was at your father's wedding. May your life be like his—an existence marked by sobriety and honour—and your death as tranquil. (*To Mrs Wilson*) Mrs Wilson, I remember your sweet daughter, when but a child of nine years, and that seems only yesterday. (*To Edward and Mary*) May you live in happiness for the rest of your days.

Music 23 ends

Music 24: Villain Theme (during Cribbs' Speech)

Cribbs enters DL

Cribbs (*aside*) Little hope of that, I dare swear, if my plan goes smoothly. Ha! Ha! Ha!

Cribbs exits DL

Miss Spindle enters D R

Act I, Scene 5

21

Miss Spindle (*aside*) I don't think I can bear it a moment longer. My beloved Edward married to that stupid little Mary Wilson. But I'll get my own back. They'll regret this day. You see if they don't.

Miss Spindle exits DR

Mrs Wilson My dearest children, may the blessing of a bereaved heart, rest, like the dews of Heaven, upon you. Come, friends and neighbours, this is a festival of joy. Be happy, I entreat you.

William (*moving CS*) Well dang me, if there be any folks here happier than William Downton, I reckon I'd like to see 'em.

Music 25: Villain theme (during Cribbs' Speech)

Cribbs enters DL

Cribbs (*aside*) But not for long—not for long. Ha! Ha! Ha!

Cribbs exits DL

William Come, lads and lasses—young 'uns and old 'uns alike—let's cheer 'em on their way.

Music 26: Wedding Day (reprise)

Edward and Mary start to move towards UR exit during song. The rest of the company move to L or R to clear the way

All   Ding dong, ding dong,
                  What a very merry time.
                  Ding dong, ding dong,
                  Hear the wedding bells all chime.

During the last verse, Edward and Mary reach UR, turn, and are showered with rose petals by the company. The scene ends with them waving goodbye, and all the company waving to them

                  Ding dong, ding dong,
                  We all wish them well today,
                  Ding dong, ding dong,
                  On their happy wedding day,
                  On their wedding day.

CURTAIN

Music 27: Entr'acte ("A Mother's Love" into "I'm A Charmer")

ACT II

SCENE 1

The interior of Miss Spindle's house — a few weeks later

Miss Spindle is seated in the armchair R. Cribbs standing on her left

Cribbs Now, dear madam, this is a most serious affair — breach of promise. Pray acquaint me with the fullest particulars of the whole, shocking business.

Miss Spindle Oh, sir, why will you cause me to harrow up my feelings, my bleeding heart by the recital of my afflictions? I have let concealment, like a caterpillar on a buddleia tree, feed on my muslin cheek ... and ... and ... (*aside*) I can't remember the rest of it.

Cribbs Alas, poor lady, pray go on.

Miss Spindle The first time I came acquainted with the gentleman was at the annual Harvest Home. Not that I make a practice of attending such vulgar festivities, Squire, but——

Cribbs Oh, certainly not — certainly not.

Miss Spindle Well, I was over-persuaded. I bound up two stooks of corn, Squire——

Cribbs (*moving to behind table*) Indeed, indeed, I will make a note of that. (*He sits, and writes in his note book*) It may be a matter of vital importance. You are certain it was but two stooks? It is best to be particular. We shall make out a prima facie case.

Miss Spindle Yes, Squire — two. Well, it so happened that the second of the two stooks I bound was — as fate would have it — the last to be bound on the farm, and so custom had it that I must be — kissed. Oh, Squire, think of my mortification, when I was told that such was the invariable rule — the custom at Harvest Home.

Cribbs Your suffering must have been intolerable.

Miss Spindle Oh, sir, you know how to feel for delicate timidity. A big, coarse young man called Arthur Bullock, rose up to snatch the fragrance from my unwilling cheek——

Cribbs (*groaning*) Oh!

Miss Spindle I put up my kerchief — it was a fine linen, Squire Cribbs, and said I had a choice in these matters — looking at Edward, whom I took to be a gentleman, you know. He took the hint immediately. Bullock fell back appalled at my manner, and Edward — oh, sir — spare my blushes!

Cribbs (*leaning forward*) Go on! Go on! Tell me!

Miss Spindle (*simpering*) He — he — did it, sir. I felt the pressure of his warm lips on — on ——

Cribbs Your cheek, of course.

Miss Spindle Oh, no, no, sir. As the poet says — it was from my lips he stole ambrosical blisses.

Act II, Scene 1

Cribbs Enormous! Enormous!

Miss Spindle The sun that set upon that terrible day was not more red than was my burnished cheek.

Cribbs I am not sure, Miss Spindle, but I think we might make out a case of assault and battery.

Miss Spindle It was exceedingly rude for a man of his education and breeding. Well—after that—after that—he bowed to me, one morning, as we were coming out of church.

Cribbs Aha! The evidence comes in. (*Making notes*) Have you any proof of that, most injured fair one?

Miss Spindle (*rising and moving towards Cribbs*) Oh, sir—no proof would be required. I trust that a person of my respectability need bring no proof of what they know.

Cribbs Well, I would not be so certain that——

Miss Spindle But what of the cow?

Cribbs (*aside*) First a bullock and now a cow—what can she mean? (*Aloud*) Cow, Miss Spindle?

During Miss Spindle's speech Cribbs writes furiously

Miss Spindle Yes, indeed. (*Moving DRC*) I was on my way down to Mr Simons and, lo, a cow stood in the middle of the High Street. I must pass within a few feet of the ferocious animal if I continued on my intended route. As luck would have it, Edward came down the lane by the blacksmith's and witnessed my strait. He saw that I stood trembling like some fragile flower tossed by the winds of heaven. (*She rushes across L*) Like Sir William Wallace flying to the rescue of the Greeks, he came panting on the wings of love. (*She rushes back R*) He rushed, like an armed castle, to the side of the cow (*turning to face C*), and she wheeled about like the great Leviathan of the deep, and trotted down towards the village school.

Cribbs I can imagine your feelings, Miss Spindle—a delicate young lady in imminent danger.

Miss Spindle You may judge what were the emotions of my palpitating heart, tender as it always was——

Cribbs Have any letters passed between you?

Miss Spindle Oh, yes, yes! Five or six, sir.

Cribbs Splendid, splendid! (*He makes notes, closes his book, and rises*) We've got him there, aha! If Miss Spindle would be so condescending as just to show me one of those letters.

Miss Spindle But he has them all in his possession.

Cribbs Horrible! How did he obtain possession of those letters?

Miss Spindle I sent them—sometimes by one person, sometimes by another.

Cribbs How, madam? *His* letters, I mean—how did he get——

Miss Spindle Oh, sir, mark his ingratitude. I sent him half a dozen and——

Cribbs Yes, yes!

Miss Spindle Not one letter did he write to me—not one.

24   The Drunkard

Cribbs (*discouraged*) The correspondence was all on one side, then?

Miss Spindle Alas, yes. Think of it—all my tenderness, all my devotion. Oh, Edward—as the immortal bard has said—thou hast sliced my heart in twain.

Cribbs (*aside; moving slightly DS*) And she is an immortal bore if ever I met one. (*Aloud*) Well, good day, Miss Spindle. I have just recalled a most pressing engagement for which I am already several minutes late. I——

Miss Spindle But Squire—what is your legal advice? How ought I to proceed?

Cribbs (*turning to face Miss Spindle*) Do you really want me to tell you, Miss Spindle?

Miss Spindle (*taking one pace towards Cribbs*) Oh, yes, indeed—indeed, yes.

Cribbs Then Miss Spindle, I would suggest that you proceed along the upper lane until you reach Farmer Thompson's big meadow——

Miss Spindle (*one pace nearer to Cribbs*) Yes?

Cribbs Then walk across to his farmyard, and——

Miss Spindle (*one more pace*) Yes, yes?

Cribbs When you get to his big, green pond——

Miss Spindle (*facing Cribbs*) Yes? Yes? Yes?

Cribbs Jump in, go down thrice and come up but twice. Good day to you.

Cribbs exits L

Miss Spindle Spirit of Lucretia Borgia! How dare he speak to a gentle lady like that? (*She runs after Cribbs*) Squire Cribbs, come back here at once! I demand satisfaction—Squire Cribbs!

Miss Spindle exits L

The Lights fade to Black-out

Music 28: I'm A Charmer into Now I've Found Thee

SCENE 2

The leafy lane—ten years later

Mrs Gates, a middle-aged woman enters R. At the same time, Mrs Stevens, another woman of the same age, enters L. They are both carrying shopping baskets. They cross, and then turn to face each other

Mrs Gates Good day to you, Mrs Stevens.

Mrs Stevens Good day, Mrs Gates.

Mrs Gates (*leaning towards her*) Have you heard?

Mrs Stevens I don't listen to tittle-tattle. (*She puts down her basket, and leans towards Mrs Gates*) What is it?

Mrs Gates (*in a stage whisper*) It be about Mr Edward.

Act II, Scene 2

Mrs Stevens Yes?

Mrs Gates (*looking off-stage to make sure no one is listening*) They do say he was not in church last Sunday.

Mrs Stevens (*shocked*) Never!

Mrs Gates Oh, it's true enough.

William enters L and moves behind the women to listen to their conversation

Mrs Stevens Well, I'm right sorry. We used to consider Mr Edward a most promising young man, and when we saw him get married and settle down in the cottage with his pretty young wife, we thought to have a respectable man like his father for a neighbour.

Mrs Gates For a neighbour.

Mrs Stevens And him with as pretty a young daughter as ever you'd wish to meet.

Mrs Gates As ever you'd wish to meet.

Mrs Stevens But now——

Mrs Gates But now——

Mrs Stevens I earnestly hope he doesn't stick to these bad ways.

Mrs Gates These bad ways.

William (*coming between them*) I don't exactly know what 'ee means, Mrs Stevens. Mr Edward is about the same free, kind-hearted fellow as he were ten year ago when he got wed.

Mrs Gates Ten year ago when he got wed.

William Why, bless me if, this very morning, he didn't tell I to go to Ned Grogan's the tailors and get I measured for a new suit of clothes at his expense. Now if I, as is his foster brother and sees everything as he do —if I thinks well of him, I don't know as other folks needs to be so perpendicular about it.

Mrs Stevens All right then. I'll tell you what I heard. (*She looks round to make sure they are alone*).

William Go on, then.

Mrs Stevens Do you know that Squire Cribbs says that if your foster brother doesn't attend a little more to his own interests——

William He'll do it for he, I suppose. Now, Mrs Gates, if 'ee wasn't a lady, I'd tell 'ee straight what I thinks of that sly old fox of a cunning Squire Cribbs. But as 'ee's a lady, I mustn't tell 'ee, must I?

Mrs Gates Indeed, no (*She starts to move off L*).

William (*running after her and bringing her back to C*) So I won't tell 'ee that, in my opinion if Mr Edward's soul was put in a great box, that seven thousand souls like that there black beetle's wouldn't fill up the spare room round the edges.

Mrs Gates Round the edges. But for all that, William, I fear that Mr Edward is in a dangerous way. They say he spends his sabbaths going about all over Hertfordshire from one public house to another. Now, I'm not saying he does drink too much—but there are a great many that have begun that way.

Mrs Stevens Alas, yes.

William Well, goodbye to 'ee—and thank 'ee.
Mrs Stevens Goodbye, William.
Mrs Gates Goodbye, William.

Mrs Gates exits L; Mrs Stevens R

William I don't think Mr Edward drinks too much—at least I hopes not. For my part, I wishes he'd never seen nothing stronger than milk or green tea. Oh, I wished I'd never seen them two women. They make I feel as bad as ever just as I was athinking I was getting over it, and beginning to see daylight again. What, dear Mr Edward with such a sweet lamb of a wife and the prettiest young 'un as ever drew breath—oh, no—it be nothing. All it were as he did was to take a bit of a bowl of punch with a friend down at *The Flying Horse*. That be no more nor no less than (*he looks L then R; in a stage whisper*) the Parson do. All the same, I reckons it be better let alone altogether—for they do say as if a man don't put his hand into the fire . . .

Introduction to Music 29 begins

 . . . he do stand a better chance of not burning his fingers.

Music 29: Old Devil Temptation

There's some as likes brandy and some as likes gin,
And others as thinks that all drinking's a sin.
But I've got my own brand of philosophy
I reckons won't never do no harm to me.

Act II, Scene 2

(*He moves C*)

Let the cat have her mouse and the dog have his bone,
But I leaves old Devil Temptation alone.

There's some as likes dark girls and some as likes fair,
And others, I reckons, as don't really care.
But just let one catch you and you'se good as dead,
And 'fore you can argue, you finds yourself wed.

(*He moves L*)

Let the cat have her mouse and the dog have his bone,
But I leaves old Devil Temptation alone.

There's some as likes silver and some as likes gold
While others wants nothing at all, I am told.

(*He moves C*)

But I likes what I'se got and don't want no more,
And while I'se got that I can't never be poor.
Let the cat have her mouse and the dog have his bone,
But I leaves old Devil Temptation alone.

(*He moves to exit L*)

But I leaves old Devil Temptation alone.

William exits L

The Lights fade to Black-out

Music 30: Old Devil Temptation into **Down With Demon Drink** (slowly)

SCENE 3

Interior of the Village Inn—two years later

There is a bar R. There is a settle L facing the audience, with a table in front of it. One or two villagers are seated on the settle. Sam Adams is standing by the bar US end; the Landlord is behind the bar cleaning some tankards. Sam bangs his empty tankard on the bar

Sam Draw I another pint of beer, Landlord.

Landlord And how are you going to pay for it?

Sam Same as I always does. Just 'ee write it down on the slate.

Landlord The slate be full up, Sam Adams. It's covered from top to bottom with your name. Rub off old scores, and I might think about it. In the meantime, you can save your breath in asking for more in my house.

Sam (*grumbling, and sitting on right end of the settle*) It comes to a fine thing when a decent man can't get no credit in the house he nigh on lives in—that it do.

28   The Drunkard

Edward Middleton enters L, dressed rather shabbily

Edward walks to the bar

Edward Give me some brandy. How much, Landlord?
Landlord (*pouring brandy*) A sixpence, sir. This is something superior; a
   bottle I keep for those who are willing to pay a little more. Are you
   quite well, sir?
Edward (*drinking*) Well, quite well, I thank you. (*He finishes the brandy*)
   This is good, Landlord. Another glass, if you please.

Music 31: Villain Theme (on entrance of Cribbs)

Cribbs enters DL

Cribbs (*aside*) Ah, ha! Who do we have here? Mr Middleton! Now to
   arrange his downfall. (*Aloud; moving to Edward*) Why, Mr Middleton.
   I'm delighted to see you. First time I was ever here—except on business
   of course.
Edward (*turning to face Cribbs*) I . . .
Cribbs Your first time too, I'll be bound—of course, of course. Why this
   is fine. Now, my young friend, since we have met each other, we'll
   honour the house. What say you?
Edward I . . . I . . .
Landlord Squire, how are you? Glad to see you. What is it to be, gentle-
   men? The same, Mr Middleton?
Edward I beg you to excuse me. You know I have just drunk. Never do
   I allow more than two glasses to pass my lips in one day. In that way
   do I remain within the bounds of sobriety.
Landlord Why, Squire, it must be full ten years and more since I last saw
   you. Do you remember the occasion?
Cribbs I cannot say that I do.
Landlord But you must remember, Squire. I saw you digging behind that
   tree and I asked what you were burying and——
Cribbs (*letting out a violent shriek and moving DR of bar*) Ah, ah, ah!
Edward (*to his L*) What is it? Are you ill?
Cribbs (*making a remarkable recovery*) Only the cramp. I am subject to it.
   (*Aside*) How much does the fool suspect? (*Aloud*) Come, let's drink,
   Edward, and I refuse to take no for your answer.
Edward (*moving to C*) I cannot. I must not.
Landlord Oh, take a little more, Mr Middleton. The Squire wouldn't ad-
   vise you to what wasn't right.
Cribbs (*moving to DS end of bar*) Come—here's whisky—good whisky.
Edward I believe I drank——
Landlord Mr Middleton drank brandy before.
Cribbs Not half so healthy as good whisky.
Edward But I——
Cribbs What's the matter with you, man—are you afraid?

Act II, Scene 3

Edward (*moving back to US end of bar*) Afraid? I? Whisky be it. It can't be stronger than the other was.

Landlord Very well, gentlemen. (*Pouring drinks*) Here you are then, two measures of the best whisky.

Cribbs Thank you, Landlord. (*He takes the drinks and gives some money*)

Edward Thank you. (*He drinks*) Well, this is pleasant. Ah, this goes to the right spot, eh, Cribbs? Is this Scotch whisky?

Landlord That it is—none better. Made with the pure water of the Highland streams.

Edward Let us drink to that (*raising his glass*) to the waters of the Highland streams, and all the noble people of Scotland. (*He drinks*)

Cribbs Hear! Hear!

Villagers Hear! Hear!

Music 32: Villain Theme

Cribbs (*aside*) Now is he started on the road to ruin. He had the taste for drink already—it needed but a gentle push to send him tottering over the edge of sobriety into the abyss of dipsomania. Ha! Ha! Ha!

Music 32 ends

(*Aloud*) But your glass is empty. (*He moves back to the bar*) Let me get you another.

Edward I ... I ... why not?

Cribbs Why not, indeed. Landlord, fill my friend's glass. No—wait. (*He puts a soverign on the counter*) Here, I'll purchase the bottle. (*He takes the bottle and pays for it*)

Landlord As you say, Squire. Thank you kindly. (*He gives change*).

Cribbs (*pouring a large measure into Edward's glass and a minute portion into his own*) Let us drink to all our friends.

Edward (*raising his glass*) To all our friends. (*A little tipsy*) You are my friend, Cribbs. (*Leaning towards him*) You've always been my friend. I never doubted it.

Cribbs Never.

Edward I have a heart, Cribbs—(*more tipsy*) I have a heart. More whisky, Cribbs? More whisky?

Landlord crosses to Villagers to collect tankards

Cribbs In a moment or two. I still have this one unfinished.

Edward (*ignoring Cribbs' remark and filling Cribbs' glass and his own*) Come—a bumper. Here's the health of my old, tired friend, Cribbs. (*He drinks*)

Cribbs (*throwing away the drink, unseen by Edward*) To my old friend, Edward!

Edward Landlord. Landlord!

Landlord (*moving to L of Edward*) Sir?

Edward We know how to do the handsome thing, Landlord.

30

The Drunkard

Landlord That we do, sir—that we do.

Cribbs fills Edward's glass while he is talking to the Landlord

Edward (*picking up his glass*) Well, I think, Landlord, a little spirit hurts no man.

Landlord Oh, no, sir. Does him good, in fact. (*He returns behind the bar*)

Edward (*moving down to Cribbs—his arm round his shoulder*) I have a heart, Squibbs—a heart, my old boy. Come let's have another horn. (*He picks up the bottle and lurches to C. To Sam*) Why don't you join us, old sulky?

Sam I drinks when I'm dry. Good English beer, I drinks. You can keep your spirits and such like.

Edward You're saucy, old fellow—that's what you are.

Sam Go away—you be making a fool of yourself, you be.

Edward (*moving to R of Sam*) A fool! Say that again, and I'll knock you down—a fool!

Sam (*rising*) I want nothing to say to you—be off—you're drunk.

Edward Drunk? Death and fury!

Edward strikes Sam who falls back on to the Villagers

Sam (*rising and moving to Edward*) Take that, then!

Sam strikes Edward who falls back and is caught by the Landlord

Music 33: Villain Theme (fast)

Edward and Sam struggle and fight. The Landlord tries to part them while the onlookers cheer. Cribbs moves to the exit R

Cribbs (*aside*) Just as I planned it. My scheme has worked out only too well. Now he is lost—lost! Ha! Ha! Ha!

Cribbs exits R

Sam (*breaking free and getting a bottle from the bar*) Take that and that!

Sam hits Edward on the head with the bottle, who falls CS with his feet towards the audience. Music 33 finishes

I was not to blame. He asked for that, Landlord.

Sam exits R

Landlord Well, he's got it anyway—serve him right—quarrelsome young fool. House was quiet enough till he came in disturbing honest people. This is too bad. How to get this fellow home? He lives two miles from here at least.

William enters L and crosses right across stage stepping over Edward without seeing him

William Mr Middleton! I have a message for 'ee. I—where be 'ee? (*He does a double take*) Lordy, what be this? (*He seizes Landlord*) Be it 'ee

Act II, Scene 3

as done this to poor Mr Middleton, eh? If it be 'ee, I'll take 'ee apart, that I will.

Landlord Let go my throat.

William Who did it? Tell I! Tell I!

Landlord Let go! It wasn't me. It was Sam Adams.

William throws off the Landlord who moves away L to the Villagers

William Very well—I'll let 'ee off this time. (*He kneels beside Edward*) There be blood on his forehead. Mr Edward, speak to me—oh, speak! What be going to happen to his poor wife and to poor sick Mrs Wilson too?

Edward (*reviving*) Where am I? What is this? What's been the matter here?

William Don't 'ee know I, sir? It be poor William, come to help 'ee. I heards as how 'ee were in a row at the inn and I comes straight here to take 'ee home.

Edward Ah, now I think I remember. Where are they all? (*He sits up*) Where's Cribbs?

William (*to Landlord*) Cribbs! Were he here?

Landlord Er—yes. The Squire was here for a short while. (*Moving to L of Edward*) Can you walk, sir?

Edward (*getting up*) Walk? Yes, I can walk. What's the matter with my head? Blood!

Landlord Don't you remember Sam Adams?

Edward Sam Adams? What the devil have I been about?

Landlord Why, Adams said you were drunk, and you hit him, and he struck you on the head with a bottle.

William Bottle was it? (*Aside*) If I gets hold of that Sam Adams, I'll bottle he—I'll pickle he—that I will or my name be not William Dowton! (*Aloud—turning to face Edward*) Come along, Mr Edward. Come along home.

Edward Drunk! Fighting! Oh, shame! Shame!

William (*moving to R of Edward*) Just 'ee lean on me, Mr Edward—lean on me. (*To the Landlord*) And 'ee go and sand thy sugar, and water thy bad brandy—old corkscrew!

The Landlord moves L to the Villagers

His poor wife! His poor wife!

Edward Hush, William, hush!

William I wishes I had died afore I seed this—that I do.

Edward Drunk! Fighting!

Music 34: Villain Theme (slowly)

My wife! My child! Oh, agony! Agony!

William, with Edward leaning on him, exit R

The Lights fade to Black-out

32   The Drunkard

SCENE 4

The leafy lane—several months later

Cribbs enters L

Cribbs So far the scheme works admirably. Day by day, he sinks deeper
into the gulf of disgrace and ruin. I know his nature well. He has tasted,
and will not stop short now of madness or oblivion.

Music 34 finishes

Music 35: He Has Fallen

(*Standing CS*)   He has fallen, he has fallen,
                     Fallen down so low.
                     Now he's fallen, now he's fallen,
                     I won't let him go.

(*He moves DR*)   He's my victim, he's my victim.
                     He'll soon cringe and cower.
                     He's my victim, he's my victim,
                     Helpless in my power.

(*He moves UC*)   He is drinking, he is drinking.
                     Watch him swill it down.
                     He is drinking, he is drinking.
                     I will let him drown.

(*He moves DL*)   He is wretched, he is wretched.
                     What a wicked thirst.
                     He is wretched, he is wretched.
                     Drink had done its worst.

Act II, Scene 4

(*He moves CS*) He has fallen, he has fallen.
He'll be at my feet.
He has fallen, he has fallen.
Ah, revenge is sweet!
Ah, revenge, revenge is sweet!

(*Looking off L*) I mostly fear his wife. She has great influence over him. Ah, who's this? William Dowton! I will retire and listen to find what he is about. (*He hides behind the tree R*)

William enters R and moves CS

William Ah me, what's to be done? Poor Mr Edward has been drinking again. I went to meet him to help him home, but he told I as how he wanted to walk on his own for a bit to sober he up afore he goes home to his poor wife and child. Ever since that day when he had that fight with old Sam in the inn, he be a proper devil for the drink, and that be a fact. I'se lost count of the number of times I'se had to carry he home. Poor old Mrs Wilson takes on most cruel, too, and she be so very, very ill. (*He looks off R*) Ah, here he comes. I'll hasten on, for if he sees I, he'll be angry and swear I be watching him. That old serpent Cribbs (*he makes a threatening gesture*) he'd better keep away from I for I'd think no more of wringing his old neck than I would of twisting that of a tough old hen.

William exits L

Music 36: Villain Theme

Cribbs (*coming out from behind tree looking cautiously to make sure William has gone*) I'm much obliged to you, most valiant William Dowton. I shall hold myself *non est inventus*, I assure you. Ah, here comes Middleton. Caution! Caution!

Cribbs hides offstage

Music 36 ends

Edward enters R

Music 37: Now I've Found Thee (slowly)

Edward Is this to be the issue of my life? Ever since that dreadful day in the inn when that scoundrel Cribbs tempted me, have I been lost. (*He moves CS*) Oh, must I ever yield to the fell tempter? Why, surely I have eyes to see, hands to work with, feet to walk, and brains to think. Yet the best gifts of Heaven I abuse, lay aside her bounties, and with my own hand, willingly put out the light of reason. I recollect my mother said — my dear dying mother — they were the last words I ever heard her utter — "Whoever lifts his fallen brother is greater far, than the conqueror of the world".

34 The Drunkard

Music 37 ends

Oh, how my brain burns! My hand trembles! My knees shake beneath me! I cannot, will not appear before them thus. A little—a very little—will revive me and strengthen me. (*He looks off L and off R*) No one sees. William will be there ere this. Now, for the hiding place. Oh, the arch cunning of the drunkard! (*He goes behind the tree and brings out a bottle; looks around again and drinks*) So! So! It relieves. It strengthens.

Cribbs appears from where he has been hiding off L and stands DL

Music 38: Villain Theme (briefly)

Cribbs (*aside*) Glorious! Glorious! As I suspected, he is a secret drinker.
Edward Oh, beautiful, beautiful liquid! Why did I rail against thee? Ha! Ha! (*He empties the bottle*) All gone! All! (*He throws away the empty bottle*) Of what use the casket when the jewels have gone? Ha! Ha! I can face them now. (*He sees Cribbs*) Cribbs here? Confusion! I have not set eyes on him since that fateful day.
Cribbs (*moving L of Edward*) Why, Edward, my old friend, my dear friend, what means this?
Edward (*pointing with outstretched arm*) Tempter! Begone! Pretend not ignorance. Were you not there when I started on the road to ruin? Did you not desert me and have I not lived a life of utter wretchedness ever since?
Cribbs As certain as I am an honest man, I know not what you mean. Business called me out. I left you jovial and merry with your friends.
Edward Friends! Ha! Ha! The drunkard's friends! Well, well, you may speak truth—my brain wanders. I'll go home. (*Moving R*) Oh, misery, misery! Would I were dead.
Cribbs Come, come. A young man like you should not think of dying.
Edward You are a single man, Cribbs. You do not know what it is to see your little patrimony wasted away—to feel that you are the cause of sufferings you would die to alleviate.
Cribbs Pooh! Pooh! Suffering! Your cottage is worth a hundred sovereigns at least. It was but yesterday that Farmer Benson was inquiring how much it could be bought for.
Edward Bought for! Cribbs, I . . .
Cribbs Well, Edward, well?
Edward (*pointing off L*) You see yon smoke curling up among the trees?
Cribbs Yes, Edward. (*Pointing off L*) It rises from yon cottage.
Edward You know who lives there?
Cribbs Why, you do.
Edward And who else, Cribbs?
Cribbs Your family, to be sure.
Edward And you counsel me to sell it! You advise me to take the warm nest from that mourning bird and her young one—to strip them of all that remains of hope or comfort, to make them wanderers in the wide world—and for what? To put a little pelf into my leprous hands, and then to squander it on drink.

Act II, Scene 5

Cribbs You do not understand me, Edward. I am your sincere friend. Believe me, come ...

Edward (*pushing past Cribbs*) Leave me—leave me!

Cribbs Why, where would you go thus, Edward?

Edward (*pointing off L*) Home! Home! To my sorrowing wife—her dying mother and my poor, poor child.

Cribbs But not thus, Edward—not thus. Come to my house. We'll go in the back way—no one will see you, and I'll give you a little—something to refresh you. I'll take care it shall not hurt thee.

Edward (*aside*) Ought I? Dare I? (*Aloud, to the audience*) Shall I go? Shall I? (*To Cribbs*) Is it indeed best?

Cribbs To be sure it is. If the neighbours see you thus, it will not be for the best. I'll take care of you. Come, a little brandy—good, good brandy.

Edward (*moving slowly towards Cribbs*) Well, I ... I ...

Cribbs That's right—come.

Edward moves nearer to Cribbs

Music 39: Villain Theme

(*Aside*) He's lost! Lost!

Music 39 ends

(*Aloud*) Come, my dear friend—come.

Edward and Cribbs exit R

The Lights fade to Black-out

Music 40: Villain Theme into Heroine Theme "B"

SCENE 5

Interior of the cottage as in Act One, Scene One. Some weeks later.

The furniture is now very plain. The tablecloth, chair covers, flowers, etc. are missing. Mary is seated in the armchair. Her dress is plain and patched but neat and clean. She is weeping

Mary Oh, Heaven aid me ! Strengthen me! Weigh not thy poor creature down with woes beyond her strength to bear. Much I fear my suffering mother never can survive the night, and Edward comes not. And when he does arrive, how will it be? Alas, my poor lost husband! ... Oh, misery—this agony of suspense—it is too horrible.

Julia enters L. She is a child of eleven. Barefooted, poorly dressed but clean. She goes to L of armchair and kneels

Music 40 ends

36   The Drunkard

Julia Mother! Dear Mother, what makes you cry? I feel so sorry when you cry. Don't cry any more, dear Mother.
Mary (*putting her arm around Julia*) Hush, child, hush.
Julia When I see you cry it makes me cry too. Will it make Father cry too, Mother?
Mary Hush, dear one, hush! Alas, he is unhappy enough already.
Julia Yes, poor Father! I cried last night when he came home, and was so ill. Oh, he looked so pale, and when I kissed him goodnight, his face was as hot as fire. This morning he could not eat his breakfast, could he? What makes him ill so often, Mother?
Mary Hush, sweet one!
Julia And dear Grandma so sick too. The doctor and the nurse both looked so sorry. Will Grandma go to Heaven tonight, Mother?
Mary (*rising*) Father of mercies! This is too much. (*She weeps*) Be very quiet, Julia. I am going in to see poor Grandma. Oh, Heaven, sweet solace of the wretched heart, support me! Aid me in this dreadful trial!

Mary exits R

Julia (*rising, moving to C*) Poor, dear Mother! When Grandma dies, she'll go to Heaven I am sure, for she is good.

The Introduction for Music 41 begins

Parson Heartall told me so, and he always tells the truth, for he is good too.

During the introduction to the song Julia moves to the table and collects the bible and returns to DSC

Music 41: Those Who Are Good

Act II, Scene 5   37

Chorus   Those who are good must win in the end.
            That's what my Daddy's big book tells.
            Those who are good to Heaven will wend
            To live in the sky with the angels.

Verse (with book open)
            Though sometimes I wonder if things will come right,
            And sometimes I'm filled full of sorrow,
            I know that the rainbow is just out of sight,
            And sunshine will come back tomorrow.

Chorus (closing book and moving to DRC)
            Those who are good must win in the end.
            That's what my Daddy's big book tells.
            Those who are good to Heaven will wend
            To live in the sky with the angels.

During the last two lines of the previous chorus, Julia returns to the table. At the end of the chorus she puts the book on the table and stands in front of the table for the next verse

Verse   And, so if I'm truthful and don't ever sin,
            The strength of my virtue will arm me.
            For those who are wicked, I know cannot win,
            And nothing that's bad can ere harm me.

Chorus (she moves DSC and kneels)
            Those who are good must win in the end.
            That's what my Daddy's big book tells.
            Those who are good to Heaven will wend
            To live in the sky with the angels.
            To live in the sky with the angels.

Julia stretches her arms upwards at the end of the song

   William enters L

William Julia, where be thy mother, darling?

Julia runs to him, puts her fingers on her lips and points to the exit R

   Ah, here she be.

   Mary enters

William (*crossing to Mary*) How be poor Mrs Wilson, now?

Mary Near the end of all earthly trouble, William. She lies in broken slumber. But where is my poor Edward? Have you not found him?

William Yes, I found him. He were in the ... in the village. I says to him, says I "Come on home, Mr Edward" I says, but he says as how he wants to walk home by his self.

38   The Drunkard

Mary Faithful friend. Was he—oh, what a question for a doting wife—was he sober, William?
William I cannot tell a lie. I reckons as how he'd had one or two—but he'll be right as ninepence—just 'ee see if he ain't.

Edward is heard singing off L

Mary Oh, merciful heavens!

William rushes out L

Julia runs to Mary

William enters with Edward who is drunk and noisy

William tries to support Edward but he staggers away to the table and clutches at it. William moves away DL

Edward I've had a glorious time, Bill. I met old ...
Mary Hush, dearest!
Edward Why should I be silent? I am not a child. I ...
Mary My mother, Edward—my poor mother!
Edward (*sinking into a chair*) Heaven's wrath on my hard heart. I forgot. Poor, poor woman! How is she?
Mary Worse, Edward, worse. (*She tries to hide her tears*)
Edward And I, in part, the cause. Oh, horrid vice! William, I remember my father's death-bed. He had faith in his heart, hope in his calm blue eyes, a smile upon his lips. He had never seen his Edward drunk.
Julia (*crossing to Edward*) Father, dear Father! (*She tries to kiss him*)
Edward Leave me, child, leave me. I am hot enough already.

Julia weeps and Edward kisses her

Bless you, Julia dear, bless you. William, do you know the young elm tree by the gate in the garden of our old house?
William That I do.
Edward I was passing that way, when I was out just now, and I slipped and fell against it. (*He rises*) My father planted that tree on the very day I saw the light for the first time. It has grown with my growth. I seized an axe and felled it to the earth (*He demonstrates*). Why should it flourish when I am lost forever? (*Hysterically*) Why should it lift its head to smiling Heaven while I am prostrate? Ha! Ha! Ha! (*He sits*)

A groan is heard off, R

Mary Merciful Heaven, what is that?
William (*starting to move R*) Let I see. I reckons ...
Mary No William, I will go. Stand back! I fear I know only too well what it may be.

Mary exits R

Act II, Scene 5   39

Music 42: A Mother's Love (slowly)

William, Edward and Julia are in a tableau of anxiety

Mary enters

Mary Edward! My mother ...
Edward (*rising*) Dead?
Mary Dead.

Music 42 ends

Edward Horror! And I the cause? Death in this house and I, without doubt the means. I cannot bear this—let me fly——
Mary (*springing forward and grasping him*) Edward, dear Edward, do not leave me.
Edward Loose your hold. I must go!
Mary No, Edward, no! I will work! I will slave—anything! But do not abandon me in my misery. Do not desert me, Edward—my love—my husband!
Edward Call me not husband—rather curse me as your destroyer. Loose your arms—leave me! (*He pushes Mary to C*)
Mary William. Hold him!
William (*grasping Edward on his left*) Edward, dear brother!
Julia (*clinging to his legs on his right*) Father! Father!
Mary You will be abused. No one near to aid you—imprisoned, or something worse, Edward.
Edward Leave me! Madness is my strength. My brain is liquid flame! Loose me!

Mary starts to faint

Mary Husband! Oh, husband!

William looses his hold on Edward, runs to Mary, and catches her as she falls

Edward Ha! I am free! Free! Farewell for ever!

Edward exits L

William Edward! Brother!

Music 43: Those Who Are Good (slowly)

Julia Father! Father! (*She runs to the exit and kneels on the threshold*) Dear Father—come back! Come back!

CURTAIN

Music 44: Entr'Acte ("Those Who Are Good" into "Villain Theme")

ACT III

SCENE 1

A Street in London. Two years later

This is a front stage scene, played against a painted back cloth or traverse curtains. There is no furniture

Cribbs I wonder where that drunken vagrant can have wandered. Ever since he came to London, thanks to his inslakeable thirst and my industrious agency, he has been going downhill rapidly. Could I but tempt him to some overt act, I could line my own pockets and ensure his ruin. Ha! Here he comes. He looks most wretchedly. Money all gone and no honest way to raise it. He'll be glad to speak to old Cribbs now.

Music 44 ends

Edward enters R. His clothes are all torn and shabby

Why, is that you, Mr Middleton?

Edward Yes, Cribbs, what there is left of me.

Cribbs You do not appear much altered.

Edward Ah, Cribbs, I am lost; a ruined broken-hearted man!

Cribbs Now, Mr Middleton, allow me to lend you a crown or two. I am not very rich, you know, but you can always have the odd crown when you want it. Ask me! (*Aside*) Before sundown, he'll be a few yards nearer his grave. (*Aloud*) There—there (*offering money*). Take it—take it.

Edward (*slowly taking it, struggling with pride and necessity*) Thank you, Mr Cribbs, thank you. You are but recently from the village?

Cribbs This very morning.

Edward I hardly dare ask if you have seen them.

Cribbs Your wife and child? Oh, they are doing charmingly. Since you left, your wife has found plenty of sewing, the gentlefolks have become interested in her pretty face. She is as merry as a cricket, and your little girl blooming as a rose and as brisk as a bee.

Edward Then Mary is happy?

Cribbs (*moving away L*) Happy as a lark. (*Aside*) Little does he know she is nigh to starvation, that she has come to London to search for him, and is living in a miserable garret. Ha! Ha! Ha! (*Aloud—moving back towards Edward*) She is radiant—radiant.

Edward I am glad, although she thinks no more of me.

Cribbs Oh yes, she thinks of you from time to time.

Edward (*moving to Cribbs*) Does she indeed?

Cribbs Yes, she says that Heaven never sends affliction without the antidote. She says that, but for your brutal—hem!—your strange conduct and drunkenness—hem!—misfortune, she would never have attracted

Act III, Scene 1 41

the sympathy of these kind friends, who now regard her as the pride of their circle.

Edward Does she really say all that?

Cribbs Yes, and she pities you. I am sure she thinks of you, and would be glad to see you become once more a respectable member of society.

Edward (*musing*) It is very kind of her. Pities me! Respectable! But, Cribbs, how can a man become respectable, without a penny in his pocket or a whole garment on his wretched carcase?

Cribbs There are more ways than one to remedy these casualties. If the world uses you ill, be revenged upon the world!

Edward Revenged? But how, Cribbs, how?

Cribbs (*moving DSL; aside*) Now—now for the moment I have planned for so long. Now to use the wretched man for my own ends, and to secure his final downfall. Ha! Ha! (*Aloud*) Do you see this paper?

Edward (*to UR of Cribbs*) Yes, what is it?

Cribbs 'Tis a cheque for a thousand pounds.

Edward A thousand pounds! But I don't understand.

Cribbs I will explain. Now, I know that you are a most excellent penman. Write upon this cheque the name of Arden Rencelaw, and henceforth you may laugh at poverty.

Edward Forgery?

Cribbs An ugly word, my dear Middleton—an ugly word. Shall we say— a little deception with the aid of the pen?

Edward (*moving away C*) Call it what you will, it is nothing less than forgery—an iniquitous crime. And against whom? Arden Rencelaw— the princely merchant! The noble philanthropist! The poor man's friend! The orphan's benefactor! Out and out on you for a villain, and coward! Wretch as I am, by the world despised, shunned and neglected by those who would save and succour me, rather than that my dear child should blush for her father's crimes, I would sooner perish on the first dung hill. (*He throws down the money*) Take back your base bribe—miscalled charity! The maddening drink that I should purchase with it, would reek of a sin and be rendered still more poisonous by your foul hypocrisy.

Cribbs (*picking up the money; bursting with rage*) Ah—you say that now in the heat of your passion, but you'll think better when—when you find yourself starving!

Music 45: Villain Theme (briefly)

Cribbs exits

Edward Has it come to this, then? An object of pity to my once adored wife. Other friends have fully made up my loss. She is flourishing, too, while I am literally starving. What's to become of me? Deserted—miserable—but one resource—I must have drink—I must have drink. But how am I to purchase it? Ah—my handkerchief—'twill gain me a drink or two at all events. Whisky—ay, whisky!

Edward rushes off L

42 The Drunkard

Music 46: London Theme changing to **Villain Theme** (on Cribbs' entrance)

To denote a slight passage of time, two elegantly dressed couples enter—one couple from R and the other from L. As they meet, the gentlemen raise their hats to the ladies and bow, but after they have passed, both ladies glance back to look at the other's gown

Cribbs enters R

Cribbs Plague take the fellow! Who would have thought he would have been so foolishly conscientious? But, I will not abandon my scheme on the house of Rencelaw. The speculation is too good to be lost. I must pen the cheque myself, and trust that the deception will pass unobserved. Why, as I live, here comes that old fool Miss Spindle. What can she be doing in London?

Music 47: I'm A Charmer (Chorus)

Miss Spindle enters L, dressed in a ridiculous compound of fashions

Miss Spindle (*aside*) Why, this London is the most awful place to find one's way I was ever in. It's all ups and downs and ins and outs. I've been trying for two hours to find St. Paul's Cathedral and I can't see it anywhere, though they do say it is even bigger than our village church.

Music 47 ends

Cribbs (*crossing to R of Miss Spindle*) Why, angelic Miss Spindle, how do you do? How long have you been in the great metropolis?
Miss Spindle Oh, Squire Cribbs—what a dreadful place it is. Not at all like the village. I can't wait to get back there.

The introduction to Music 48 begins

I've seen some terrible things here, I can tell you—terrible.

Cribbs moves UC

Act III, Scene 1   43

Music 48: Pity A Girl

Miss Spindle (*moving DSL*)
    I'm up here in London to look at the sights
    And I'm simply dazzled by all of the lights.
    Oh, silly old me, how my head's in a whirl.
    It's really too much for an innocent girl.

(*She crosses DR*)
    Pity a girl up in London, dressed in her very best gown.
    Pity an innocent maiden. Pity a girl up in town.

(*Moving US of Cribbs*)
    The things I have seen are too bad to relate.
    Their frightfulness I simply can't contemplate.
    I fear if I dallied for even a trice,
    I might finish up in a black den of vice.

(*Breaking DR*)
    Pity a girl up in London, dressed in her very best gown.
    Pity an innocent maiden. Pity a girl up in town.

(*Moving C*)
    It's really not safe for a girl such as me.
    For down every alley await men, you see.
    And though I might scream till my very last breath,
    They'd whisk me away to a fate (*mouthing*) worse than death.

44   The Drunkard

(*Moving DL*)
Pity a girl up in London, dressed in her very best gown.
Pity an innocent maiden. Pity a girl up in town.

(*Moving C*)
Pity a girl up in London, dressed in her very best gown.
Pity an innocent maiden. Pity a girl up in town.

Cribbs Indeed it is a den of all the vices—not at all a suitable place for innocent, good-living people like you and me.
Miss Spindle Quite—quite. By the by, Squire, can you tell me what has become of the Middletons? She left the village some months ago.
Cribbs Ah! I've had my eye upon them, never fear. They're down, Miss Spindle—down, never to rise again. As for that vagabond, Edward Middleton ...
Miss Spindle Ah, Squire! What an escape I had! How fortunate that I was not ruined by the nefarious influence, the malignant coruscations of his illimitable seductions. How lucky that prim Mary Wilson was subject to his hideous arts, instead of my virgin immaculate innocence!
Cribbs Quite—quite. I'll tell you something further about Miss Mary Wilson—or Mrs Edward Middleton as she is now to her cost. She is here—in London.
Miss Spindle No!
Cribbs Indeed she is. The foolish girl declared that she would sooner follow her drunken husband than remain, where she was, without him.
Miss Spindle Oh, she is low—degraded! Do you know she sank to taking in washing to feed herself and her child. And she is with him now?
Cribbs No—she has been unsuccessful in her search for him. But I know where he is. 'Tis but a few minutes since I parted company with the wretched man.
Miss Spindle Really!
Cribbs And I know where she is living. (*Aside*) I must pay her another visit before long. (*Aloud*) Which way are you going, did you say? Towards St. Pauls? Allow me the exquisite honour of escorting you there. Your arm, lovely and immaculate Miss Spindle.

Cribbs and Miss Spindle move arm in arm to the exit L

(*Aside*) They say the old fool is loaded with money. If I play my cards right, I may extort some from her.

Cribbs and Miss Spindle exit

The Lights fade to Black-out

Music 49: Pity A Girl (chorus) into **Though He Has Left Me**

Act III, Scene 2 45

SCENE 2

Music 49 ends

A wretched garret in a poor district of London. The next day

The furniture consists of an old table and a broken chair. There are no curtains at the window and the only light is from an old lamp which burns dimly on the table RC. Mary, in miserable apparel, is seated L of the table, sewing, a shawl thrown over her shoulders. Julia is sleeping on a straw bed on the floor DL, covered, in part, by a ragged blanket. There is half a loaf of bread on the table

Mary Alas! It is very cold. I am faint with hunger. I am sick and heart weary with wretchedness, fatigue and cold.

A clock strikes one

One o'clock, and my work not near finished. These shirts have I promised to hand in tomorrow by the hour of eight. A miserable shilling will repay my industry, and then, my poor, poor child, thou shalt have food.
Julia (*waking*) Oh, dear Mother, I am so cold.

Mary rises, takes the shawl from her shoulders, crosses to Julia and spreads it over her

(*Giving the shawl back to Mary*) No, Mother—keep the shawl. You are cold, too. I will wait till morning, and I can warm myself at Mrs Duncan's fire. (*She goes to sleep murmuring*)

Mary waits till Julia is asleep and then places the shawl over her and returns to her chair

Music 50: Heroine Theme "B" (slowly)

Mary Alas, where is he on this bitter night? In vain have I made enquiry, and cannot gain any tidings of my poor, lost husband. Perhaps he is the inmate of a prison. Oh, merciful Heaven, restore to me my Edward, and I will endure every ill, that can be heaped upon me. (*She looks towards Julia*) Poor Julia, she sleeps soundly. She was fortunate today, sweet lamb. While walking the streets in search of wood for the fire, she became benumbed with cold. She sat down on some steps, when a boy, moved with compassion, slipped a few pence into her hands. The mother of that boy is blessed! She purchased a loaf of bread and ate part of it.

Music 50 ends

(*She takes the loaf from the table*) The rest is here. (*She rises and looks at it eagerly*) I am dreadfully hungry. I shall have money in the morning to buy another loaf in its place. (*Pause*) No—no, my child will wake and find her treasure gone. I will not rob my darling. (*She replaces the loaf on the table*)

The introduction to Music 51 begins

That ever I should see his child thus! For myself, I could bear, could suffer all.

Music 51: Though He Has Left Me

Mary (*C*)

    Though he has left me
    Lonely, neglected and poor,
    I know that he'll return
    One day for evermore.

(*Moving DRC*)

    Though through temptation
    Terrible errors he's made,
    He'll find the sober path
    From which he has but strayed.

(*Returning to C*)

    He was my darling,
    Never duty he'd shirk,
    Until that fateful day
    The bottle did its work.

    Drink was his downfall.
    I pray this evil will cease.
    If all men would sign the pledge,
    Then we could live in peace.

Act III, Scene 2   47

Julia (*kneeling up on her bed of straw*)
                        Hear all the children,
                        Ragged and starving they cry,
                        "Close down the Public House
                        And Demon Drink will die".

Mary crosses to Julia

Mary   (*together*)
Julia
                        Hear all the children,
                        Ragged and starving they cry,
                        "Close down the Public House
                        And Demon Drink will die".

Julia Dear Mother, you are cold. Take back the shawl.

Mary (*on her knees*) Now Heaven be praised, I did not eat that bread.

Julia Why do you sit up so late, Mother? Mother, do not cry. Is it because Father does not come to bring us bread? We shall find Father, bye and bye, shan't we, Mother?

Mary Yes, dearest—yes, with the kind aid of Heaven.

There is a knock at the door. Mary rises. Julia scurries back to bed and hides under the bedclothes

A knock! Who can that be? Ah—could it be Edward!

Music 52: Villain Theme (briefly)

Cribbs enters R

Cribbs (*moving below the table*) Your pardon for my intrusion at this untimely hour, but friends are welcome at all times and seasons, eh? So, so, you persist in remaining in these miserable quarters. When I last saw you, I advised a change.

Mary Alas, sir, you know too well my wretched reasons for remaining here. But why do you come at this strange hour? Have you brought joyful tidings of my Edward?

Cribbs (*avoiding a direct answer*) I must persist in it—you would do well to remove elsewhere.

Mary Return to the village, I will not. I must remain in London and find my husband.

Cribbs This is a strange infatuation. He has others to console him whose soft attentions he prefers to yours.

Mary What mean you, sir?

Cribbs That there are many women—not of the most respectable class— who are always ready to receive presents from wild young men, and are not very particular in the liberties that may be taken in exchange.

Mary (*moving away L*) Man, man, why dost thou degrade the form and sense Heaven has bestowed on thee by falsehood? (*Pointing to Julia*) Gaze on the sharp features of that child, where famine has already set

48 The Drunkard

her seal. Look on the hollow eyes and the careworn form of the hapless being that brought her into life. Then, if thou hast heart further insult the helpless child, and the wretched wife.

Cribbs These things I speak of, have been, and will be again, while there are wantons of one sex and drunkards of the other.

Mary Sir, you slander my husband. It is because he is poor, forsaken, reviled and friendless, that thus I seek him, thus love him still.

Cribbs Ha! Ha! Ha! He would laugh in his drunken ribaldry, to hear you talk thus.

Mary (*with proud disdain*) Most contemptible of earth-born creatures, it is false!

Cribbs Tut! Tut! You are very proud, considering—(*he looks round the room*)—all circumstances. (*Moving to Mary*) But come, I forgive you. You are young and beautiful, your husband is a vagabond. I am rich. I have a true affection for you, and with me—(*he attempts to hold her*).

Mary Unhand me, you wretch! (*She throws him off*) Have you not proved yourself a slanderer, and to effect your own vile purposes? But know, despicable wretch, that my poor husband, clothed in rags, covered with mire and lying drunk at my feet, is a being the laces of whose shoes you are not worthy to unloose.

Cribbs Nay, then, proud beauty, you shall know my power—'tis late, you are unfriended, helpless—and thus——

Cribbs seizes Mary. Julia screams

Music 53: Villain Theme (fast)

Mary Help! Mercy! I am undone!

Mary struggles with Cribbs, breaks free and runs across the room. Cribbs follows her and grabs her again. Julia runs and tries to drag Cribbs away

William rushes in R

William seizes Cribbs and throws him to the ground. Mary and Julia cling together

Music 53 ends

William (*his foot on the fallen Cribbs*) Well, Squire, what be the lowest you'll take for your rotten carcase? Shall I turn auctioneer, and knock 'ee down to the highest bidder? (*Giving Cribbs a push with his foot*) Be off, 'ee ugly varmint or I'll make 'ee into mincemeat—that I will.

Cribbs (*getting to his feet*) I'll be revenged, if there's law or justice!

William Oh, get out afore I knock 'ee down again!

Cribbs Let me tell you, I am a man who ...

William You a man! Nature made a blunder, I reckon. Her had a piece of cow dung her meant to form into a pig, but her made a mistake, gave it your shape, and sent it into the world to be miscalled man. Get out!

William pushes Cribbs off R. A loud crash is heard

Act III, Scene 3   49

Mary and Julia rise

William enters

William I did not like to hit him afore you, but I reckon as how he's gone
down them stairs a fair sight quicker than he come up 'em.
Mary Kind, generous friend, how came you here so opportunely?
William Well, I'll tell 'ee. I was just going to my bed at a lodging house
nearby Angel Street when I happens to mention to the landlord about
'ee. And would 'ee believe it—he knew where 'ee was. I thought as how
'ee might be more comfortable there, and his good wife has made everything as nice and as pleasant for 'ee as if 'ee was her own sister. So,
come along, Mrs Middleton, back with I to these kind folks, and bring
the young 'un with 'ee.
Mary (*with both arms outstretched*) Dear, kind William. How can I ever
thank you?
William No need for that, I be certain.
Mary What brings you to London, William?
William Why, to look for 'ee and Mr Middleton, of course. Come along
then to my lodging and when I'se got 'ee safely there, I'll continue my
search for Mr Edward. Just 'ee rest assured, I'll find thy husband, if I
have to search the length and breadth of London town!
Mary Heaven bless you, and preserve my poor, dear Edward.
William Come!

The Lights fade to Black-out

Music 54: Though He Has Left Me into **Down With Demon Drink** (slowly,
ending on opening of scene three)

SCENE 3

A street in London. Early the next morning. It is still only half light

Edward is lying on the ground C, clothes torn, eyes sunk and haggard

Edward (*waking*) Where am I? I wonder if people dream after they are
dead. Hideous! Hideous! Early morning—the rosy hue of the coming
sunshine, veiling from mortal sight the twinkling stars ... what horrid
dreams—will they return upon me, waking? Oh, for some brandy!
Whisky! I am not so ashamed—so striken with despair, when I am
drunk. Give me some brandy! What street is this? ... Pain! ... dreadful
pain! Heavens, how I tremble! ... Brandy! Landlord ... Brandy! (*He
sinks down in agony*)

The Landlord enters right, carrying a whip

Landlord Where in nature can my horse be gone?
Edward Hello! Landlord, I say!
Landlord What's that? (*Aside*) Well, as I live, if it isn't that reprobate

50   The Drunkard

Middleton. I will pretend I do not observe him. (*He starts to move off R*)

Edward Landlord! Wait! I know you. We have been acquainted before now, eh, Mr ...

Landlord (*aside*) Zounds! He knows me. (*Aloud*) Yes, yes, we were acquainted once. But that was in other days.

Edward You are the same being still—though I am changed—miserably changed. You still sell whisky, don't you?

Landlord I am a respectable landlord.

Edward Respectable! You speak as if you were not the common poisoner of the whole village. Am not I, too, respectable?

Landlord (*laughing loudly*) Not according to present appearances. You were once as so was Lucifer! Ha! Ha! Like him you have fallen past rising. What has brought you to this beastly condition, young man?

Edward (*springing up and pointing an accusing finger at the Landlord*) You! Demon Drink!

Music 55: Down With Demon Drink

Edward
Chorus
Down with Drink! Down with Drink!
Down with Demon Drink!
Listen all—heed my call
Down with Demon Drink!

Verse
There were days, long ago,
When I was a man.
Now I've sunk just as low
As a human can.

Act III, Scene 3   51

Landlord
Chorus
Down with Drink! Down with Drink!
(*He mimes drinking*)
Down with darling drink!
Hear me cry—come and buy!
Down with darling drink!

Verse
At my Inn I've a store
Of all kinds of wine,
Lots of ale, lots of beer.
Drinking it is fine.

Edward
Verse
Give it up! Give it up!
Drinking is a sin.
Landlord
Drink it down! Drink it down!
Whisky, rum and gin.

Both
Chorus
Down with Drink! Down with Drink!
Down with Demon Drink
Darling
Hear our cry! Hear our cry!
Down with Demon Drink
Darling

Edward (*moving away L*) How looked I when I first entered your loathsome den, and how do I look now? Where is my wife? Where is my child? They have cursed me, and forsaken me.

Landlord Well, what brought you to my house? I did not invite you, did I?

Edward (*turning to face the Landlord*) Doth hell send forth cards of invitation to its fires of torment? I am sick and faint—make me some amends—my brain is on fire. My limbs are trembling—give me some whisky—whisky! (*He seizes the Landlord*).

Landlord How can I give you whisky? My inn is thirty miles from here. I am on a visit to London to see my sister. Let me go, vagabond!

Edward Nay, I beseech you—only a glass—a single glass of whisky—brandy—rum—anything. I have a claim on you—a deadly claim! Whisky! Whisky or I'll throttle you. (*He starts to choke the Landlord*)

Landlord (*struggling*) Help! Murder! I am choking! Help!

William enters R

William (*aside*) Lordy me, what be this? Why it be Edward! I have found him at last. Praise be to Heaven! But what be he doing? (*Aloud*) Edward! Edward!

52   The Drunkard

Edward releases the Landlord and falls to the ground

Landlord You shall pay for this, villain. You shall pay for this.

The Landlord exits

Edward (*in delirium*) Here—here, friend ... take it off, will you ... these snakes ... how they coil about me. Oh, how strong, they are ... there .... no, no, don't kill it—give it whisky, poison it with brandy. That will be a judicious punishment ... that would be justice ... ha! ha! Justice. Ha! ha!

William He do not know I.

Edward Hush! Gently! Gently, while she's asleep. I'll kiss her. She would reject me, did she know it—hush! There ... Heaven bless my Mary, bless her and her child ... hush! If the globe turns round once more we shall slide from its surface to eternity. Ha! Ha! Great idea ... a boiling sea of wine, fired by the torch of fiends! Ha! Ha!

William He be quite helpless, and that's a fact. I must try to gain some assistance. I reckons he's quite safe here. He can't move as to injure hiself. I will run for timely aid.

William exits R

Edward So—so—again all is quiet. They think I cannot escape. I cheated them yesterday. 'Tis a sin to steal drink ...

Arden Rencelaw, the elderly philanthropist, enters L

... but no crime to purloin sleep from the apothecary—none ... none. (*He produces a phial*) Now for the universal antidote—the powerful conqueror of all earthly care—death!

Edward is about to drink when Rencelaw seizes the phial and throws it off stage

Rencelaw Nay, friend—take not your life—but mend it.

Edward (*rising*) Friend, you know me not. I am a fiend, the ruin of those who loved me—leave me—leave me.

Rencelaw I come not to upraid, or insult you. I am aware of all your danger, and come to save you. You have been drinking.

Edward That you may well know. Even now, am I dying for drink. If, as you say, you are my friend, then give me whisky, whisky! Who are you that takes interest in an unhappy vagabond—neither my father nor my brother?

Rencelaw I am a friend to the unfortunate. You are a man, and if a man, you are my brother.

Edward You trouble yourself without hope. (*He moves away*) I am lost. Of what use can I be to you?

Rencelaw Perhaps *I* can be of use to *you*. Are you indeed a fallen man.

Edward looks at him, sighs and hangs his head

Then have you the greater claim upon my compassion, my attention, my utmost endeavours to raise you, once more, to the station in society

Act III, Scene 3

from which you have fallen. "For he that lifts a fallen fellow creature from the dust is greater than the hero who conquers a world".

Edward (*starts and moves away*) Merciful Heaven! My mother's dying words! (*He turns*) Who and what are you?

Music 56: Those Who Are Good (softly)

Rencelaw I am one of those whose life and labours are passed in rescuing their fellow men from the abyss into which you have fallen. I administer the pledge of sobriety to those who would once more become an ornament to society, and a blessing to themselves and to those around them.

Edward It cannot be. I have sunk too low for redemption.

Rencelaw You see before you one who, for twenty years, was a prey to this dreadful folly.

Edward (*moves towards Rencelaw*) Indeed! (*He checks and turns away*) No! No! It is too late.

Rencelaw It is not. Come with me. We will restore you to society. Reject not my prayers. Strength will be given to you. (*He moves to left exit and turns to Edward with outstretched hands*) Come, my brother—enrol your name among the free, the disenthralled, and become a man once more.

Edward (*moving to take Rencelaw's outstretched hands*) Merciful Heaven! Grant the prayer of a poor wretch be heard.

Edward and Rencelaw exit L

Music 56 ends

Music 57: Villain Theme (briefly)

Cribbs enters R

Cribbs Now for my design on Rencelaw and Co. I think there can be no detection. The signature is perfect ... although it be I that say it. I'll get some well-dressed boy to deliver the cheque, receive the money, and I'm off to America. Would I were certain of the ruin of the drunken scoundrel Middleton, and the infamy of his tiger-like wife, I should be content indeed. (*Looking off R*). There is a likely lad to run my errand to the bank. (*Calling*) Boy! Boy, come here! Do you wish to earn yourself a half florin?

The Lights fade to Black-out

Music 58: Villain Theme into Though He Has Left Me (ending on opening of scene four)

54   The Drunkard

SCENE 4

The London street — the next morning

William enters from the left, Rencelaw from the right. They meet C

Rencelaw Ah, honest William. I have been searching for you. Edward desires to see you.

William Thank 'ee, sir and bless 'ee. How be Edward, and where be he?

Rencelaw At my home and reasonably well and happy. Now, William, I am making arrangements to send his wife and child back to their cottage in the village. I will send a carriage to your lodging, to take them home, this very morning. Their happy home is prepared for them, and I have obtained almost certain information of his grandfather's will.

William Thank Heaven!

Rencelaw I will proceed to the village later today with Edward, but there are grave matters which delay my immediate departure from London. A forgery was committed yesterday, in the name of our firm, upon the City Bank.

William Bless me — the City Bank — a forgery! Who gave the cheque, sir?

Rencelaw 'Twas a boy, William — a young boy.

William What time of the clock, yesterday, would it be?

Rencelaw Why, a little after the bank opened in the morning. Why this eagerness?

William I ... I'll tell 'ee, sir. Mr Middleton told I that Lawyer Cribbs, when poor Mr Middleton was in poverty and drunkenness, urged he to commit a forgery and, dang me, if, yesterday morning, I didn't see old Cribbs give a boy a cheque, and tell he to take it to the City Bank, get some money, and bring it to he in Fore Street. Now, sir, I reckons as how I ain't extra bright, but I thinks I can fathom out old Cribbs' wicked plan.

Rencelaw And so can I, indeed! I see it all. (*He moves to the R exit*) Come with me to Bow Street and secure an officer of the law. Come!

William If once I get my grip on the old fox, I reckons he won't get easily loose — that he won't. I'll follow 'ee, sir, heart and mind.

Rencelaw Come then!

William exits with Rencelaw

The lights Fade to Black-out

Music 59: Down With Demon Drink into **Now I've Found Thee** (ending on opening of scene five)

SCENE 5

Exterior of the cottage — that afternoon

Mrs Miller is seated on the bench in front of the tree DRC, Mrs Gates is on her right, and Mrs Stevens on her left

Act III, Scene 5

Mrs Stevens Has 'ee heard the news, Mrs Gates?

Mrs Gates What news be that?

Mrs Stevens Why, about Squire Cribbs. They do say he has committed a heavy forgery on the City Bank up in London.

Mrs Gates Well I hope, for the credit of the village, you be mistaken and he be not guilty of this bad action.

Mrs Miller Have I not always said that his heart was blacker than his coat? Witness his conduct to the sweetheart of poor Will's sister, Agnes.

Mrs Stevens Have you not heard?

Mrs Miller What?

Mrs Stevens About Agnes—her senses have been restored.

Mrs Gates Never!

Mrs Miller Good Doctor Wordworth always said her malady was but temporary.

Mrs Stevens They say the poor girl has some secret that she'll not tell to anyone but William—not even to Mary, although she be back home in her own cottage again with her sweet little daughter. (*She looks towards the cottage*)

Mrs Gates Sweet little daughter. Ah, 'tis a happy day indeed. She will soon be reunited with her beloved husband who has been rescued from sin by the kind Mr Rencelaw.

Mrs Miller They do say, Mr Edward will be back here this very afternoon.

William enters L

Mrs Stevens Ah, William. 'Tis nice to see you back in the village, after all your adventures in London.

William (*moving L of the women*) Thank 'ee kindly, Mrs Stevens.

Mrs Gates Are Mr Middleton and Mr Rencelaw not with you?

William No—they be up on the top lane. That old fox Cribbs has come back to the village, but he's slipped from our grasp.

Mrs Stevens (*backing to R of Mrs Gates*) Oh!

William Don't 'ee be afraid, Mrs Stevens. Us'll catch the old rogue, 'ee can be sure. Mr Middleton and Mr Rencelaw be up on the top lane and there be an officer of the law at the cross-roads and I be here—so I reckons he'll not escape us.

Mrs Gates Have you seen your sister, William?

William No, I ain't seen the poor girl. Nor will—not till this rogue Cribbs be in our clutches.

Mrs Gates But she wants to see you. She has some secret to tell you.

William Secret! It be some of her wild fancies, I reckons.

Mrs Stevens William, you are mistaken. Your dear sister's mind is quite restored.

William What! How? Don't 'ee trifle with I, Mrs Stevens. I could not bear it.

Mrs Stevens I tell you, William, she is quite sane—quite well.

Mrs Miller As Doctor Wordworth said she would be.

William (*to C stage*) What! Will her know I and call I by my name again? Shall I hear her sweet voice carolling to the sun at early morning? Shall

56   The Drunkard

I once more at evening hear her murmur the prayers our poor old
mother taught her? (*Turning to the three women*) Thank Heaven! Thank
heaven!

Agnes is heard singing off L

Mrs Gates Why, William, she's coming.

Music 60: Those Who Are Good (softly)

Agnes enters L plainly but neatly dressed

Agnes (*seeing William*) William! Brother!
William My darling little sister!

William and Agnes embrace

Agnes I know you, William. I can speak to you, and hear you, dear
brother.
William May heaven be praised for this!
Agnes I have much to tell you, and 'tis important that you should know
it instantly. Edward is on his way back here, and it concerns him most.
When I recovered my clear senses—when I remembered our old home,
and Buttercup, the little brown cow I used to milk, and Neptune and
could call them by their names . . .
William Bless you!

Music 60 ends

Agnes Strange fancies would keep forming in my brain, and remembrances
flit along my memory like half-forgotten dreams. But among them was
a vague thought that, when insane, I had concealed myself and seen
something hidden. Searching round carefully, I saw a little raised hillock
behind that tree over there. I went and fetched a spade from Farmer
William's barn, and after digging near a foot below, I found—what
think you, William?
William What, girl, what?
Agnes An old tin case and, concealed within, the will of Edward's grand-
father confirming to his dear son the full possession of all his property.
The other deed under which Cribbs has acted was a forgery . . .
William Where is it now?
Agnes (*takes a purse from around her waist*) I have it here.
William Give it to I.

Agnes hands the purse to William

Just 'ee wait till Edward sees this. But here he be now—and
Mr Rencelaw and the Officer with he.

Rencelaw, Edward and the officer enter

Rencelaw Friend, William, Cribbs is coming down the hill carrying a

Act III, Scene 5   57

spade. Quickly hide—all of you. Let us observe him, and see what business he has in mind.

William Come along then. Now, old Cribbs, I reckons I knows what he be looking for, and I reckons that all 'ee'll get will be a hornet's nest about thy ears.

They all hide—William and the Women DR. The others UL

Cribbs enters L, carrying a spade

Music 61: Villain Theme (slowly)

Cribbs (*looking behind him*) All's safe. I'm certain no one has observed me. Now for the will. From this fatal evidence I shall at least be secure. (*He moves behind the tree*) Powers of mischief—the earth is freshly turned. (*He searches*) The deed is gone! (*He leaves the spade by the tree*)

Music 61 ends

Agnes enters L in a feigned madness

Agnes (*chanting*) The will is gone—the bird has flown
The rightful heir has got his own.
Ha! Ha! Ha!

Cribbs (*paralysed*) Ha! Betrayed! Ruined! Mad devil, you shall pay for this.

Music 62: Villain Theme (fast)

Cribbs rushes at Agnes. She runs across round the stage twice, pursued by Cribbs

William enters R and catches Cribbs' arm and holds up the will. The Officer enters L and seizes the other arm and points a pistol to Cribbs' head. Rencelaw DLC holds up the forged cheque and points to it. The others all point at Cribbs. Tableau

Music 62 ends

William Trapped! Trapped! Why I'll . . .

Rencelaw (*moving to L of the group*) hush, William, hush! Do not oppress a poor down-fallen fellow creature. (*To Cribbs*) Unhappy wretch. This world's goods were plenty with you. What tempted you into these double deeds of guilt?

Cribbs Revenge and avarice. I hated the father of Edward Middleton. In early life he detected me in an act, that might have cost me my life. He would not betray, but pardoned and pitied me. From that hour I hated him with feeling of intensity that has existed even beyond the grave, descending unimpaired to his beloved son. By cunning means, I wormed myself into the favour of the grandfather, who, in his dying hour, delivered into my hands his papers. I and an accomplice forged false papers, leaving all the property to me. The villain who assisted me, left

58   The Drunkard

the country. Fearful he should denounce me, should he return, I dared
not destroy the true will. But yesterday, news reached me that the villain
had died. And now, one blow of evil fortune has destroyed me.
Rencelaw Repentance may yet avail you.
Cribbs No. I have lived a villain—a villain let me die!

Music 63: Villain Theme (fast)

*Cribbs knocks the pistol out of the Officer's hand, and rushes off DR
followed by the Officer, blowing his whistle, and all the others on stage at
this time. They all shout "Stop him", "Don't let him get away", "Villain"
etc. At the same time all the rest of the cast (except Mary, Julia, Miss
Spindle and, of course, Mrs Wilson) are waiting in the wings DL and tag
onto the end of the line so that there is a continuous line of people chasing
across the front of the stage. Before there is any break in the chase, Cribbs
runs on from DL, realises that he is caught in both directions, and the
officer picks up his revolver and points it at Cribbs. The whole company
who have been involved in the chase come on stage and shout "Trapped"*

Music 63 ends

Officer Come along, you.

Music 64: Villain Theme (very slowly)

Cribbs exits with the Officer, slowly

Music 64 ends

William Oh, Mr Rencelaw, what blessings can repay 'ee?
Rencelaw The blessings of my own approving conscience. "The heart of
the feeling man is like the noble tree, which, wounded itself, yet pours
forth precious balm."
William Well, if there be a happier man than William Dowton, I reckon
I'd like to see he. My brother Edward again a man, (*he goes to Edward*)
and my dear sister restored to me.

Agnes goes to William and there is a general embrace

Music 65: Now I've Found Thee (softly)

William and Agnes break to L of tree

Edward (*breaking away*) And now—where is my dear, my loved, my faithful wife? (*He knocks on the cottage door*)

The door opens and Mary comes out followed by Julia

Mary Edward, my dear, dear husband!

Mary and Edward embrace

Edward Mary, my blessed one. (*To Julia*) My child, my darling!

Act III, Scene 5

59

Julia Father, dear Father, you look as you did the bright, sunshiny morning I first went to school and you kissed and blessed me. Do not cry, Father. But your tears are not such tears as Mother shed, when she had no bread to give me.

Edward (*kissing Julia*) No, my blessed child, they are tears of repentance—tears of joy.

Mary Oh, my beloved—my redeemed one! All my poor sufferings are as nothing, weighed in a balance with my present joy.

Music 65 ends

Edward (*going to Rencelaw*) What gratitude do I not owe to this generous, noble-hearted man, who, from the depths of wretchedness and horror, has restored me to the world, to myself, and to religion? Respected sir, what words can express our gratification?

Rencelaw Pay it where 'tis justly due—to heaven! I am but the humble instrument, and in your happiness am I rewarded.

Julia (*going to Rencelaw*) I shall not forget what Mother taught me last night.

Rencelaw What was that, sweet child?

Julia (*kneeling R of Rencelaw*) In my prayers, when I ask a blessing for my mother and father, I pray to heaven to bless Arden Rencelaw too.

Rencelaw (*putting his hand on her head*) Dear child.

Edward I will not wrong your generous nature by fulsome outward gratitude for your most noble conduct, but humbly hope that heaven will give me strength to continue in the glorious path of sobriety, adorned by your bright example.

All Amen!

The whole company on stage sing:

Music 66: Those Who Are Good (reprise)

All
Those who are good have won in the end.
Just as her Daddy's big book tells.
And, at life's end, to Heaven they'll wend
To live in the sky with the angels.

Though sometimes they wondered if things
would come right,
And sometimes were filled full of sorrow,
They knew that the rainbow was just out of sight,
And sunshine would come back tomorrow.

Our story's done and virtue has won,
Just as her Daddy's big book tells.
The moral's clear—keep off rum and beer

60   The Drunkard

And you'll finish up with the angels.
The moral's clear—keep off rum and beer
And you'll finish up with the angels.

CURTAIN

Curtain Call (Entire Company)

Music 67: Reprise of Songs

Wedding Day
Ding dong, ding dong
What a very merry time.
Ding dong, ding dong,
Hear the wedding bells all chime.

Ding dong, ding dong,
We all wish them joy today,
Ding dong, ding dong
On their happy wedding day
On their wedding day.

Down with Demon Drink
Ladies   Give it up! Give it up!
              Drinking is a sin.
Men   Drink it down! Drink it down!
              Whisky, rum and gin.
All   Down with Drink! Down with Drink!
              Down with Demon Drink!
              Hear our cry, hear our cry!
              Down with Demon Drink!

Pity a Girl
Pity a girl up in London, dressed in her very best gown.
Pity an innocent maiden. Pity a girl up in town.
Pity a girl up in London, dressed in her very best gown.
Pity an innocent maiden. Pity a girl up in town.

Though He Has Left Me
Hear all the children. Ragged and starving they cry,
"Close down the Public House and Demon Drink will die".
Hear all the children. Ragged and starving they cry,
"Close down the Public House and Demon Drink will die".

Those Who Are Good
Our story's done and virtue has won,
Just as her Daddy's big book tells.
The moral's clear—keep off rum and beer

Act III, Scene 5   61

> And you'll finish up with the angels.
> The moral's clear—keep off rum and beer
> And you'll finish up with the angels.

The whole company raise their arms as if to heaven, but in fact to draw attention to a slogan which descends from above, bearing the legend:
"THE THEATRE BAR IS NOW OPEN"

CURTAIN

Music 68: Play-Out Music (repeat of Overture)

PRODUCTION NOTES

STYLE OF PERFORMANCE

The difficulty we encounter when we set about producing a melodrama is that, whereas we understand that the less sophisticated audiences of the 19th century accepted them with a fair measure of credulity, it would be almost impossible to expect a modern audience to take them seriously. How then should a producer tackle them for presentation today?

The first solution might appear to be to burlesque them unmercifully. I do not agree with this method of approach. This style of presentation might work for a short extract or, perhaps, for a one-act melodrama, but for a full evening's entertainment the joke wears thin very quickly. I have found that the most successful way is to overplay them—that is to say, to use the style of acting we now label 'ham' and to very slightly burlesque those passages where the dialogue is too absurd to be treated in any other manner. But it is very important to remember that the audience must never be aware that you are laughing at the characters being portrayed. It is the high seriousness of the play which causes hilarity. Another thing to look out for is the juxtaposition of overstatement with understatement which should get good laughs. An example is the outburst of Edward in Act 1, Scene 2, which is followed by Cribbs' line: "I perceive you are put out."

Movement and gesture should be exaggerated rather like the old silent films. A convention of melodrama rarely used in the modern play is the aside. There are several ways of treating this, but boldness should be the key. The aside given in a stage whisper, with the back of the hand shielding the actor's mouth from the other players can be amusing and can be used occasionally, but by far the most laughs are achieved by the actor who breaks away from the characters to whom he is speaking and approaches the footlights and addresses the audience directly while everyone else on stage "freezes" for the duration of the aside, in whatever position they are in at the time. A good example of this occurs in Act 3, Scene 3, when Edward is choking the Landlord and William enters and has his aside, leaving the two players in an absurd "freeze", before he goes to the rescue. Situations like this occur throughout the play, and the more ridiculous the position the actors are left in during the "freeze", the funnier it is.

The temptation to play melodrama slowly must be avoided at all cost. There should be a good overall pace so that the audience are not allowed to realize how absurd the situation is before they are whisked on to the next improbability.

To sum up, I would say—paint the scenes boldly with broad strokes, exaggerate, caricature, and do not be afraid of overstatement. To the actor I would say that if you underplay you may be certain that the audience will laugh at you rather than at the character you are portraying; but if you play the part with all the stops out, if you treat this as that unique

Production Notes 63

opportunity to overact almost unreservedly, then not only will you enjoy yourself, but you may be sure that the audience will, too.

CASTING AND NOTES ON THE CHARACTERS

The number of parts in this version is very flexible. There are 8 speaking parts for women and 7 speaking parts for men (one of these has only one line!). By doubling and excluding the non-speaking parts, it is possible to reduce the size of the cast to 7 women and 5 men, but for companies wishing to utilise a large number of actors, the size of the cast could be as large as you wish.

Cribbs   should be suave and plausible when he is addressing the other characters but thoroughly evil and nasty in his asides. He is rather older than most villains in melodrama, but should not be played as a "stage old man".

Edward   should be handsome, likeable and charming in the earlier scenes and, even when he is on the downward path, should retain the audience's sympathy. He makes a remarkable recovery in Act 3, Scene 5, and should appear as he did at the opening of the play.

Mary   is the typical heroine of melodrama—sweet and rather naive to begin with, and when she has been deserted by Edward, must bear the burden of her troubles without appearing to be a "moaner", or the audience will become unsympathetic.

Miss Spindle   is "mutton dressed up as lamb" and affects coyness and modesty. She considers herself to be a lady, and overdoes the "refainment". She often uses the wrong words, and is not very certain about her H's.

William   is the "Tim Bobbin" character so well-loved by Victorian audiences. He is not quite so simple as he seems, and is always at hand to rescue anyone in distress. He should be played very sympathetically, and the audience will love him.

Mrs Wilson   the typical heavy of melodrama. The part needs to be overplayed but, as with Mary's later scenes, she must not appear too much of a "Moaner".

Julia   is a young girl of 11—a favourite character of melodrama. She typifies simplicity, and is absolutely ingenuous. It is not necessary that the part should be played by a child—indeed, rather like Juliet, it requires an experienced actress to play the part successfully. A small actress, with a long blonde wig, satisfies an audience completely.

Agnes   is a small part but her mad scene (which has much in common with that of Ophelia) can be very effective, even if it is only very slightly overplayed.

Landlord   a fairly straightforward part—reasonably jovial in his

	first scene in his own inn, but less sympathetic in his other scene in London.
Rencelaw	the blandly, generous philanthropist who turns up late in the play to restore the hero to sobriety and his family. The part needs to be played "big"—particularly in the delivery of his homilies.
Sam Adams	elderly, but not too old to be able to engage in the fight with Edward.
Mrs Gates Mrs Stevens Mrs Miller	just country folk who like to gossip. Small parts, but quite a lot of laughs if played with spirit and attack.

SETTINGS

This play has been written in such a way that alternate scenes can be played in front of traverse curtains or drop cloths, thus reducing the time taken to affect a scene change to a matter of a few seconds. All the settings are very simple—see illustrations.

The four interiors used in the Swan Theatre production were achieved in the following manner:—Four triangular bases were made measuring 4 ft on each side. Onto these were built triangular boxes made of standard 8 ft. by 4 ft. hardboard sheets. Tops were put on to them, as the auditorium has a steep rake, but these would not be necessary in a hall with different sight lines. The boxes were fitted with castors. When three of these constructions were placed side by side they formed a self-supporting backing 12 ft. long by 8 ft. high. On these were painted the first setting. By using the fourth box, and turning round another face of two of the others, it will be seen that it is possible to produce three more similar backings— always leaving one of the boxes in the wings.

The interior settings were painted outlines on a black background so that, stood in front of a black traverse, they were very effective. In the bar scene, the boxes were set at an angle, but in the other scenes they were parallel to the footlights. Behind the back, black traverse curtains, the setting for Act 1, Scene 5, and Act 3, Scene 5, was in position permanently.

All the exits are from left to right—the only exception being in the final scene of the play when Mary and Julia come out of the cottage cut-out through a practical door, but this could be "cheated" by having the apparent door of the cottage off-stage.

There are, of course, many other ways in which the play could be staged, but the keynote should always be simplicity as it is essential that there are no waits between scenes.

MUSIC

A complete music plot appears on pages 70 and 71 and the melodies of the ten songs are printed with the lyrics in the main text of the book. In addition, every music cue is given in detail in the text at the point it occurs.

The play may be performed without the songs if required but they are

Production Notes
65

not difficult and add much to the spirit of the show. The ability to "put a song over" is more important than a good singing voice. If the songs are sung with panache, an audience is less likely to notice that a singer may be rather inexperienced.

However, even if it is decided to omit the songs in whole or part, "mood" music is essential. The full piano score includes themes for villain, heroine, etc. as well as the full arrangements for the songs. Copies may be purchased from the publishers of the play. The link music between scenes is intended only to cover the scene changes and should end as soon as the next scene is ready, except where indicated in the music plot. Often it will be possible to play only a few bars between scenes.

It must be pointed out that no alteration or addition to the music, except by way of transposition or arrangement for additional instruments, may be made without the prior permission of the publishers, who are unlikely to grant such permission except in very special circumstances. Permission is not required to omit one or more of the songs.

FURNITURE AND PROPERTIES

A full list of the furniture and props referred to in the script is given on pages 66 and 67. Producers may wish to add items of stage dressing to these but, if set changes are to be done swiftly, they are best kept to a minimum in this type of play. The only item on the front stage scenes in Acts 1 and 2 is a cut-out of a low tree—stage right. There are no items of furniture at all on the front stage scenes in Act 3.

LIGHTING

A simplified lighting plot appears on pages 68 and 69. Where there are facilities for follow spots, additional cues will be necessary. For example, it is very effective during the songs, to take the stage lighting to half and cover the singers by follow spots, cross-fading at the end of the song. A green follow spot on Cribbs on some of his entrances and soliloquies adds much to the atmosphere. If it is possible to put in old-fashioned footlights, these also help to re-create the Victorian theatre. Old dried-milk tins, cut in half, and painted black make very good imitations of the old cowl type floats.

COSTUME AND MAKE-UP

A costume plot appears on page 72. Although the period of the Swan Theatre production was described as "towards the end of the 19th century", it could be set in any period from 1840 to Edwardian.

Make-up is fairly straightforward but it should be bold with a slight tendency towards caricature for Cribbs, Miss Spindle and William.

PROPERTY AND FURNITURE PLOT

For positioning of furniture see illustrations of setting.

ACT I

Scene 1   Table covered with chenille tablecloth
2 upright chairs
1 armchair
Family bible (set on table)
Vase of flowers (or Aspidistra in pot)—set on table
Embroidery frame and silks, etc (**Mary**)
Walking cane with silver head (**Cribbs**)—throughout play
Handkerchief (**Mary**)
Handkerchief (**Mrs Wilson**)
Handkerchief (**Cribbs**)
Watch and chain (**Cribbs**)—throughout play
Draw-string purse containing money (**Mary**)

Scene 2   Cut-out tree
Purse (as previous scene)—(**Mary**)

Scene 3   Table covered with cloth
2 upright chairs
1 armchair
Stand mirror (set on table)
Toilet articles (set on table)
Paper bag of nuts (**William**)
Fan (**Miss Spindle**)

Scene 4   Cut-out tree
Money (silver crown)—(**Cribbs**)

Scene 5   2 benches
Prayer book (**Clergyman**)
Bouquet (**Mary**)
Button hole (**Edward**)
Rose petals (All except Cribbs, Miss Spindle, Edward and Mary)

ACT II

Scene 1   Table covered with cloth (no mirror or toilet articles)
2 upright chairs
1 armchair
Note-book and pencil (**Cribbs**)

Scene 2   Cut-out tree
2 shopping baskets (**Mrs Gates** and **Mrs Stevens**)

Scene 3   Bar counter
Bench or settle
2 bar stools
Round table
6 tankards
6 glasses (whisky tots)
1 brandy bottle

Property and Furniture Plot   67

          2 whisky bottles (1 empty for Sam to mime hitting Edward)
          Tray (**Landlord**)
          Cloth (**Landlord**)
          Watch and chain (**Landlord**)
          Sovereign (**Cribbs**)
          Money (**Edward**)
          Money (**Landlord**)

Scene 4 Cut-out tree
          Whisky bottle (set behind tree)

Scene 5 Table without tablecloth
          2 upright chairs
          1 armchair
          Family bible (set on table)
          Handkerchief (**Mary**)

ACT III

Scene 1 Money in draw-string purse (**Cribbs**)
          Cheque (**Cribbs**)
          Handkerchief (**Edward**)
          Parasol (**Miss Spindle**)

Scene 2 Old table
          1 broken upright chair
          Oil lamp (set on table)
          Shawl (**Mary**)
          Shirts and needle and cotton (**Mary**)
          Half a loaf of bread (Set on table)
          Bed of straw or sacking—D L
          Ragged blanket
          Handkerchief (**Mary**)

Scene 3 Whip (**Landlord**)
          Phial of poison (**Edward**)
          Cane (**Rencelaw**)
          Cheque (**Cribbs**)

Scene 4 Cane (**Rencelaw**)

Scene 5 2 benches
          Will form in purse (**Agnes**)
          Pistol (**Officer**)
          Whistle (**Officer**)
          Spade (**Cribbs**)
          Cheque (**Rencelaw**)
          Cane (**Rencelaw**)

LIGHTING PLOT

This is a list of the main lighting cues. See Production Notes on page 62 for details of additional lighting effects which can be incorporated where facilities are available

ACT I, Scene 1. Interior
To open: All lights on
Cue 1   At end of Music 9   **(Page 6)**
            Fade to Black-out

ACT I, Scene 2. Exterior
To open: Front stage area lit. Exterior daylight
Cue 2   **Edward** "My dear, dear Mary."   **(Page 11)**
            Fade to Black-out

ACT I, Scene 3. Interior
To open: All lights on
Cue 3   **Miss Spindle** "... will cling to it still."   **(Page 15)**
            Fade to Black-out

ACT I, Scene 4. Exterior
To open: Front stage area lit. Exterior daylight
Cue 4   **Agnes** exits   **(Page 18)**
            Fade to Black-out

ACT I, Scene 5. Exterior
To open: Bring up full stage area and cyclorama. Exterior daylight
No cues

ACT II, Scene 1. Interior
To open: All lights on
Cue 5   **Miss Spindle** "Squire Cribbs!"   **(Page 24)**
            Fade to Black-out

ACT II, Scene 2. Exterior

To open: Front stage area lit. Exterior daylight
Cue 6   End of Music 29   **(Page 27)**
            Fade to Black-out

Lighting Plot

69

ACT II, Scene 3. Interior

To open: All lights on
Cue 7   **Edward** and **William** exit   (Page 31)
            Fade to Black-out

ACT II, Scene 4. Exterior

To open: Front stage area lit. Exterior daylight
Cue 8   **Edward** and **Cribbs** exit   (Page 35)
            Fade to Black-out

ACT II, Scene 5. Interior

To open: All lights on
No cues

ACT III, Scene 1. Exterior

To open: Front stage area lit. Exterior daylight
Cue 9   **Cribbs** and **Miss Spindle** exit   (Page 44)
            Fade to Black-out

ACT III, Scene 2. Interior

To open: Full stage area lit—dim interior
Cue 10   **William** "Come!"   (Page 49)
            Fade to Black-out

ACT III, Scene 3. Exterior

To open: Front stage area lit dimly
Cue 11   **Cribbs** "... yourself half a florin."   (Page 53)
            Fade to Black-out

ACT III, Scene 4. Exterior

To open: Front stage area lit. Exterior daylight
Cue 12   **William** and **Rencelaw** exit   (Page 54)
            Fade to Black-out

ACT III, Scene 5. Exterior

To open: Full stage area and cyclorama lit
Cue 13   At end of Music 66   (Page 60)
            Lights up to full for Curtain Calls

MUSIC PLOT

Music No.		Page No.
1	Overture	1
2	Heroine Theme "A"	1
3	Villain Theme	2
4	Villain Theme	4
5	Chords	4
6	Song: A Mother's Love	4
7	A Mother's Love into Heroine Theme "B"	6
8	Villain Theme	6
9	Chords	7
10	Villain Theme	8
11	Heroine Theme "A"	8
12	Song: Now I've Found Thee	10
13	Now I've Found Thee into I'm A Charmer	11
14	Song: I'm A Charmer	14
15	I'm A Charmer into Villain Theme	15
16	Villain Theme	15
17	Agnes Theme	17
18	Villain Theme	18
19	Villain Theme	18
20	Bells followed by Agnes Theme	18
21	Bells into Wedding Day	18
22	Song: Wedding Day	19
23	Heroine Theme "A"	20
24	Villain Theme	20
25	Villain Theme	21
26	Song: Wedding Day (1st and last verses only)	21
27	Entr'Acte: A Mother's Love into I'm A Charmer	21
28	I'm A Charmer into Now I've Found Thee	24
29	Song: Old Devil Temptation	26
30	Old Devil Temptation into Down With Demon Drink	27
31	Villain Theme	28
32	Villain Theme	29
33	Villain Theme	30
34	Villain Theme	31
35	Song: He Has Fallen	32
36	Villain Theme	33
37	Now I've Found Thee	33
38	Villain Theme	34
39	Villain Theme	35
40	Villain Theme into Heroine Theme "B"	35
41	Song: Those Who Are Good	36
42	A Mother's Love	39
43	Those Who Are Good	39
44	Entr'Acte: Those Who Are Good into Villain Theme	39
45	Villain Theme	41
46	London Theme changing to Villain Theme	42
47	I'm A Charmer	42

Music Plot 71

48	Song: Pity A Girl	43
49	Pity A Girl (Chorus) into Though He Has Left Me	44
50	Heroine Theme "B"	45
51	Song: Though He Has Left Me	46
52	Villain Theme	47
53	Villain Theme	48
54	Though He Has Left Me into Down With Demon Drink	49
55	Song: Down With Demon Drink!	50
56	Those Who Are Good	53
57	Villain Theme	53
58	Villain Theme into Though He Has Left Me	53
59	Down With Demon Drink into Now I've Found Thee	54
60	Those Who Are Good	60
61	Villain Theme	57
62	Villain Theme	57
63	Villain Theme	58
64	Villain Theme	58
65	Now I've Found Thee	58
66	Song: Those Who Are Good	59
67	Curtain Call	60
68	Play-Out Music	61

COSTUME PLOT

Further details of costume are given in Production Notes on page 62

Mrs Wilson	Act 1 Scene 1	Black dress with shawl and lace cap
	Scene 5	The same with the addition of a bonnet
Mary	Act 1 Scene 1	Pretty dress
	Scene 2	The same with the addition of a bonnet
	Scene 5	Bridal dress
	Act 2 Scene 5	Plain, patched dress
	Act 3 Scene 2	Shabby dress and shawl
	Scene 5	Simple, neat dress
Cribbs	Throughout	Black frock coat and trousers with cloak and top hat
Edward	Act 1 Scene 2	Norfolk jacket and trousers
	Scene 5	Bridegroom
	Act 2 Scene 3	Shabby suit or as Act 1 — untidy
	Scene 4	The same
	Scene 5	The same
	Act 3 Scene 1	Torn, shabby suit
	Scene 3	The same
	Scene 5	Smart suit or could be as Act 1 Scene 2
Miss Spindle	Act 1 Scene 3	Very fussy pink dress more suitable for a young girl
	Scene 5	The same with the addition of an outrageous hat
	Act 2 Scene 1	The same (no hat)
	Act 3 Scene 1	Very fussy gown with hat and parasol
William	Throughout	Smock, corduroy trousers tied with string, soft hat
Agnes	Act 1 Scene 4	Flowing white dress
	Act 3 Scene 5	Simple dress
Mrs Miller		
Mrs Gates	Throughout	Country dresses with bonnets
Mrs Stevens		
Sam Adams	Throughout	Smock, corduroy trousers tied with string
Landlord	Act 2 Scene 3	Waistcoat, shirtsleeves, trousers, white apron
	Act 3 Scene 3	Suit, top coat and hat
Julia	Act 2 Scene 5	Child's dress—plain but neat—barefooted
	Act 3 Scene 2	White or cream nightgown
	Act 3 Scene 5	As Act 2 Scene 5 with the addition of button boots
Rencelaw	Throughout	Suit, cloak, hat
Officer	Act 3 Scene 5	Police uniform of the period
Villagers (if used)		Country suits or dresses

Lightning Source UK Ltd.
Milton Keynes UK
UKHW011828110119
335426UK00005B/558/P